Combine your heart, mind and insu... to achieve your dreams.

Disha
Pistuk

Playing
with the
Big Boys

Playing
with the
Big Boys

Success Secrets of the
Most Powerful Women
in Business

Debra Pestrak

SUN Publications

Carlsbad, California

Playing with the Big Boys
Success Secrets of the Most Powerful Women
in Business

Publisher's Cataloging-in-Publication
(Provided by Quality Books, Inc.)

Pestrak, Debra.
   Playing with the big boys : success secrets of the most powerful women in business /
Debra Pestrak. – 1st ed.
    p. cm.
   Includes bibliographical references and index.
   LCCN: 00-191671
   ISBN: 1-931034-06-0

   1. Businesswomen—Biography. 2. Women executives—Biography. 3. Success in business.
I. Title.

HD6054.P47 2001   650.1'0922
QBI00-500138

Cover design by: Ab Mobasher

Published by SUN Publications

Printed in the United States of America.

FIRST EDITION   First Printing, 2001

DEDICATION

For everyone who wants to…

Learn from the best,

Empower themselves to greater success,

and

Further their careers.

TABLE OF CONTENTS

Appendix

Playing
with the
Big Boys

FOREWORD

By Janice Roberts

General Partner—Mayfield Fund

Former Senior Vice President, 3COM and

President of 3Com Ventures

Until very recently I had followed a very similar path to the women featured in this book. For over 20 years I had worked to "climb the corporate ladder" in large U.S. and European-based companies, and I had achieved a good deal of success in both continents. Now I have joined the world of venture capital as a General Partner at Mayfield Fund, where I hope to leverage my experiences, my knowledge, and my network to create new teams and to build new companies.

In writing the foreword of this book I wanted to share with you something of my personal journey, one that has taken me from a small, sleepy village in the southwest of England to the crazy world of Silicon Valley and how that relates to the stories and experiences told here by these successful women. I decided the best approach would be to summarize some of the challenges that I have faced and the lessons that I have learned.

Firstly, I think that it goes without saying that a good and relevant education is the essential building block for any career, as it was for mine. From a relatively early age I had decided that I wanted to join the "business world," but it took me a while to find the right industry. I chose information technology, and for me this has been the best choice that I could have made, affording me the opportunity to work with some of the smartest people on the planet and in the center of the Internet revolution. My advice would be to follow new markets and go where growth is. Inevitably, there will be more opportunities and the chance to stand out from the crowd. Look at some of the women featured in this book—Ellen Hancock, Liz Fetter, and Ann Livermore have become well-respected leaders and innovators in the technology world.

Early on in my career I took an operating role, one of the best moves I ever made. I became a sales engineer with a territory and a quota, and I had the opportunity to demonstrate tangible results in a very competitive environment. I think that sales is often underrated as a career-building function. But understanding your customer, building relationships, structuring deals, and beating the competition is invaluable—and women are great at it! We focus on building relationships; we're organized; we can multitask; we are very resilient, and with a clear goal, we are unstoppable. Now, it can be hard to get an operating role because it's all too easy to be pushed into staff positions and to play a supporting role. I think that it is tremendously important to understand and contribute to the operations of a company.

I was always determined to work overseas, and I highly recommend it. Our markets today are global, and we need to understand those opportunities and how to work with people from all parts of the globe. Moving to the United States was a major challenge for me. I moved to Boston initially, for nine months, in order to build the U.S. operation for the networking company that I was managing. Ten years later I'm still here, following the sale of that company to 3Com Corporation. It was hard enough adapting to the management style of the East Coast, but moving to the West Coast two years later was a huge management challenge for me.

Many people assume that it is easier for a woman to work here in comparison to Europe, which is a more traditional environment, and I'm often asked to compare the two. In some respects it is harder here. Firstly, the business environment is much more competitive at the peer level, and there is a clear focus on individuals. Europeans, on the other hand, are much more team-oriented and prepared to mentor and coach. I found this difference very difficult at first, but instead of relying on my peers for help, I retained the services of an external coach who advised me on how to work with my peers and how to adapt my style to the high technology world of Silicon Valley. I found this support invaluable. Now I would find it very difficult to return to working in Europe, largely because the infrastructure is so much better here, and it must be said, the pay is better!

I think that our biggest challenge today—and this is not unique to women—is time, or the lack of it. Like everyone in this book, I don't have the time to do everything that I want to do. Trying to balance a family—in my case two young children—and a career is extremely hard. Certainly I could not have done this without a strong support infrastructure, both at work and home. Not a day goes by when I don't feel guilty about something. In recent years I have worked with more women in similar positions and it does help to share experiences. I often think about an interview that I read a few years ago with Carol Bartz, CEO of Autodesk. She basically said don't try to achieve balance every day—it's impossible because of the demands of the corporate world. But if you have had a busy time or an overseas trip, balance it by, for example, working from home for a few days. There is no magic answer!

Technology adds a whole new dimension to our lives. Having a home office with a high-speed computer link and a telephone with conference capabilities can add enormous flexibility to your working day. It may mean that you work early in the morning or late at night, but you can bring down travel time and spend more time with the family. I try to leverage all of the tools available to me to both optimize my time and to stay connected to my family, friends, and colleagues.

From my teens I was determined to live an interesting life, to travel the world, to become financially independent, and most of all to have a family. I've achieved those things and as a result I am happy and privileged to be part of Debra's book. In looking back over my career I don't think that I ever felt that any doors were closed to me, but there have been challenges, and it has been tremendously hard work. I have always worked with far more men than women, and in general I have not felt compromised, and I have always been able to be true to myself. Early on I decided that "I would never sell my soul in order to be successful." This is my personal mantra, and it has helped me through some difficult times.

Having learned from the lives of this group of women and from my own personal experiences, I do believe that the cost for our successes has been high. I am very optimistic about the future, and I hope that through the collective achievements of these powerful and influential women, the path is cleared for our next generation to have the confidence to take advantage of those opportunities that will be open to them.

INTRODUCTION

The Story of This Book

Have you found yourself asking:

- How can I be more successful?

- Why am I not any further along in my career?

- What don't I know or haven't I figured out about progressing in an organization?

If you've wondered about these questions, you're not alone. Neither the corporate training or seminars I'd attended, nor any of the books I'd read, gave me the answers I needed on how to excel within an organization. I could see there were a select few around me who knew something I didn't, but I couldn't seem to identify what it was. That "something" is the topic of this book. At the end of writing the book, I was surprised to learn that I'd also uncovered the secrets of being successful in anything.

Catalyst[1] (See Bibliography for all footnotes) reported in 1999[2] that there were only 375 women officers in Fortune 500® companies with profit-and-loss or revenue-generating responsibility out of 5,525 total line positions. Thus, only 6.8% of the line officers were women. ("Line" positions are those jobs that allow the jobholder to understand how the company makes money. People in these positions have the power and set the direction and policies of the company.)

The purpose of this book is to:

® Fortune 500 is a registered trademark of Time-Warner

• Share the skills and insights of women who have made it to the top so that more women can move into leadership positions and learn how to fully use their skills.

• Provide women information so they can rise above stereotypes and prejudices and take control of their own lives to achieve their goals.

• Supply information to anyone who wants to learn what it takes to advance in his or her career.

This book profiles nine of the most powerful women in American business. The criteria for being part of this exclusive group are that she:

1. Works or has worked for a Fortune 500 company

2. Holds a top position with profit-and-loss responsibility

3. Worked her way up the corporate ladder (as opposed to getting the job, for example, through family connections or as a result of a merger or acquisition.)

While women hold 375 of the total 5,525 line positions, 107 of these women hold the very top "clout" positions in their companies, *i.e.* Chairman, President, Chief Executive Office, Senior Executive Vice President, and Executive Vice President. My research uncovered less than 100 women of the 375 who fit all my three criteria. These women have figured out what it takes to succeed!

Based on the statistics, men clearly run and control the majority of companies. The focus of this book is on the women who have made it into the executive ranks and what they learned that has allowed them to excel in the male dominated business world. This book is not derogatory towards men or corporations.

There is no doubt that corporations could do more, but the fact is we need to focus on what we have control over--ourselves! Women need to step up to the plate to play the game like the big boys if they want to succeed in the corporate arena. This does not mean they need to act like a man! This is about taking our assets as an individual and using them to be our best.

What is now the subtitle was originally the title. When the title change was made, one of the interviewees chose to be removed from the book because she thought the title was sexist and could damage her career. These women have learned about adapting into their environment. The woman who withdrew was making the statement that in her environment, a book entitled "Playing with the Big Boys" would not be acceptable for her to participate in, regardless of the book content. This is an important statement on how savvy these women have to be to their surroundings. These women have worked very hard to keep their sex as a non-issue in their job performance. They are where they are because they are the right person for the job. With men controlling 88.1% of the executive positions, the title seemed an appropriate tag line.

You are about to embark on a discovery process that can change your life. This book outlines the secrets learned by the women who have made it to the top. You may choose to keep this book at your desk as a reference guide to constantly remind you of the key unwritten rules and success traits you need to succeed. For as you are about to see, these women are awesome: encouraging, inspiring, and insightful. Read and learn from them as they share their success secrets.

Chapter 1 sets the stage by describing the current status of women in the executive ranks. Chapters 2 through 11 are the edited interviews with these powerful women. Their stories are so strong and compelling that I have left them in interview format so you could hear their personal success stories directly from them. (The boldfaced, italicized portions are my questions or comments.)

The last chapter is a summary of the power plays these women learned along their paths. This is an unprecedented opportunity to use these women as mentors. Ask yourself how the skills and characteristics exhibited by these women can help you in your life. (Full Biographical Summaries of their job titles are included in back of the book so you can see what steps they took to reach the top.)

The full-length interviews on these women's success secrets are available in both audio and video formats. Ordering information is listed at the back of the book. The author, Debra Pestrak, is available to speak to corporations and organizations on this subject. Five percent of the profits from this book will be used to educate young women entering the corporate marketplace to further the continued growth of women into leadership positions.

My Story

Heading to the Division Manager's office on this sunny Tuesday morning I am struck with a sense of anxiety. He has a plush corner office overlooking San Francisco. Usually, I delight in discussing with him my latest sales strategy or successful close. But this morning my attention is focused on my female employee sitting in one of the comfortable chairs.

The previous Friday I had started to work on a performance improvement program with her, or at least *attempted* to! On Monday, I asked her to review the plan with me but she refused to meet to discuss it. As she headed for the door, I informed her if she left, a suspension would follow.

This morning she came into the office as if nothing had happened. Now the three of us are meeting in the Division Manager's office to discus the situation. Three long, grueling hours later, he decided that she would not be suspended because "she didn't hear you."

I walked up to the Division Manager afterwards and said, "Do you realize what this decision means? I have lost all credibility with my people. You've told her that as long as she doesn't hear something, that makes it OK."

Shocked, I returned to my office. *She didn't hear me.* Impossible! *I wasn't supported in my action.* Unbelievable! *We wasted three hours discussing this.* Outrageous! The blows to my credibility were undeniable.

Holding my head in my hands, I can't imagine what to do next. I'd been a successful sales manager, exceeding my targets every year and being handsomely compensated. But all I wanted to do now was to leave this position. Instead, I stayed, and the situation worsened.

Could there have been a different way to resolve the situation? Looking back, I now see how I could have acted differently before, during, and after the encounter. Responsibility with no authority is a lose-lose situation. This experience was a hard way to learn that I should not have stayed in an organization that did not support me.

There were other sales managers on the team who had employees with attitude problems. Yet when I was hired a few months before, I was the only manager directed to resolve this issue.

I learned that everyone on the management team needs to understand each other's objectives. The entire team needs to have the same vision and support each other. That is just one of several situations in my career that had me asking: What is it I don't know or understand?

Early years. Between my junior and senior year in high school, my parents moved from my school district. Because they didn't want me to change schools in my senior year, I needed a car to commute to and from school. To afford a car, I needed to get a job. Having no particular aspirations at the time, I decided to enter the corporate world as an information operator for Pacific Bell, starting at the bottom of the totem pole.

I worked in an open room with about 150 other women. It was 1970, and there were no men in these jobs. I was shocked to find out that most of the women had been there for years and quite a few who had been there 20 to 30 years. Flipping through directories improved one's alphabetizing skills, but I couldn't imagine being satisfied sitting in this spot for the rest of my career! The job worked out well for a summer job and I worked there part-time during my senior year.

I had no idea what I wanted to do with my life. My mother thought I should be a teacher. That was an acceptable path for girls. Other girls around me were either talking about marriage or going to college. I thought about going into the Peace Corps or working. Because I was going to need to pay my own way through college, I was re-thinking that option. I was not interested in having children right away. So after high school graduation, I went back to working full-time at Pacific Bell.

One day the union I belonged to went on strike. At the time, I thought supporting myself financially was more important than supporting the union. So I kept working, and that quickly put my career advancement on hold—especially because my supervisors were part of that union. I quickly learned that there were definitely rules to be followed, but not the ones written in manuals.

I was able to get a clerical position after changing job locations in 1973. Only women held clerical positions at that time. But I wanted to be in management and thought I stood a better chance of advancing through the clerical ranks.

In 1975, I was selected to be a representative at AT&T's exhibit at Disneyland. This was my favorite assignment of my career, and I hoped it would put me in a position to move into management. Unfortunately, when I rotated back to my old job, nothing materialized. Therefore, I moved to another division.

A Different Approach. As I looked up the chain of command, I didn't see any women, except those in supervisory positions like my manager. I decided my career needed a different approach, so in 1977, I attended splicing school. I learned to climb poles and twist wires together in preparation to become a splicer. This was a good-paying position held almost exclusively by men. Not many women wanted to climb poles, crawl under houses, and go into manholes. I was willing to take on a non-traditional role to reach my goals.

Right after completing splicing school, I discovered the company was looking for marketing people, and I saw this as my chance to get into management. After passing the assessment test, I went to eight weeks of training. I was the only woman among nine in the class. In fact, that was pretty much the ratio of men and women in our department. There were no women in the highest management jobs that I could look at and say, "I want her position."

Being in management brought a new phenomenon I hadn't experienced--stereotyping. As a blue-eyed blonde, I found that some people would approach me as if I had no brains. I had to work harder to prove my knowledge. To deal effectively with male colleagues and customers, first I had to reframe their perception that they were talking to a "dumb blonde." Looking young also brought challenges. During a sales call a customer might ask, "How long have you been working for Pacific Bell?" When I answered "10 years," he would relax. Many years later, I received some unsolicited advice from my (female) boss. Wear a jacket over my professional dresses, she suggested, for "more credibility." Perceptions hadn't changed much.

New career challenges brought opportunity. The telecom-munications companies were beginning to face competition on local and toll calls. The division I worked in had no plan for how it would compete. I was asked to "see what I could do" and did produce a successful plan.

Thirty days prior to the introduction of competition, another division asked me to develop and execute a similar plan. In that case, the manager had formed a team to accomplish this.

Yet none of them had my knowledge of the issues. None of the team knew me, yet they all knew each other. None worked in the same geographical area as me. When I asked the manager if I would be leading the team, she told me the team would naturally see me as the leader, but she was not going to tell them I was the leader. But I was given the responsibility for the results.

We were able to put a plan in place within the next 30 days, and it worked flawlessly. The task was accomplished, but getting it done was more difficult than it should have been. Among the lessons I learned: Different skills sets are required to lead a team at a remote location, and never take on an assignment where you are given responsibility but no authority.

After several assignments managing people, I realized my passion was working with customers. As a manager, I spent most of my time doing administrative work, planning, and strategizing. But I wanted a career that would allow me to achieve my financial goals and still stay with the customers.

While I worked for various telecommunication companies, invariably I noticed that men controlled the companies and very few women made it to the executive ranks. Why was this? I could see there was something preventing women from reaching the top. I asked myself, "What don't women know or haven't figured out that could be causing this?"

I was getting frustrated with the corporate world. It had changed a lot over the years. Yet there were other things that had not changed at all. In 1995, I attended a leadership workshop for high-potential women. After an exercise, people were asked to give each other feedback. There was a woman, a generation younger than I, who said she saw me in a different light after she heard me speak. After asking her what she meant, I saw that she had thought of me initially as a "dumb blonde." It is amazing how this stereotype gets carried from generation to generation, even among women.

The seminar gave me an opportunity to assess where I was in my career. The instructor commented that I had an entrepreneurial spirit and was surprised that I had been with a large, bureaucratic organization for so long. It seemed as if I had spent most of my career trying to think outside the box in organizations that wanted me to stay inside the box. I was not happy or satisfied in that environment and didn't see anything changing in the near future. It was time for a career shift.

On my own. I started my own seminar company in 1996, presenting motivational talks and seminars for corporations on goal achievement, success, and communication skills. I worked even longer hours, but loved it. It is very satisfying knowing that everything you do is directly related to your bottom line. This undoubtedly, is one reason people want to reach top leadership positions.

In 1998, I was writing a book on the *7 Secrets for Success*. I wanted to share what I had learned from my life experiences. In January 1999, I went away for two weeks to do nothing but finish writing *the book*. I got it all done, except for inserting the reference material. But on the way home, my computer was stolen at the airport, and the book vanished with it. This was one of the most challenging times in my life. I was depressed for several weeks. Even knowing all I know about putting myself back on my feet, I was struggling. I knew there was something I was supposed to learn from this besides backing up my computer files and keeping the disk separate. I believe that everything happens for a reason, though the reason may not be clear at the time of the event.

Though I attempted to rewrite the book, my heart was not in it. Several months later, I saw an article in *Fortune* magazine, "The 50 Most Powerful Women in American Business." The piece intrigued me. How were these women chosen for this list? What had they learned in their careers? What did they know that others hadn't figured out? It reminded me of my own experience in climbing the corporate ladder and the things I wish I had known. I went searching for books on the topic, but I couldn't locate any books about women getting to the top. What were their stories? I wanted to know more. What unwritten rules had they learned that they could share?

I, like most people, prefer not to learn things the hard way. These women had the answers. They could provide insights and words of wisdom to help anyone move up in an organization. Learning from them could eliminate a lot of frustration, anger, and heartache that many feel while trying to learn the ropes. These women could offer mentoring advice the average person would never have access to.

I started extensive research to locate powerful women who would be willing to share their stories. I wondered: How would I get in touch with these women? Would they be willing to talk with someone who was not a big name or didn't work for a television station?

Getting a Mission. I found the Catalyst web site and was amazed (or perhaps appalled) by the statistics on women officers and decided this would be my focus – women officers of Fortune 500 companies. How can Americans talk about a global economy, the accelerating rate of technology, and not be utilizing one of our largest resources – women? These statistics had to change. I had a mission.

When I started the project, I was just going to write a book. Then I realized that if I was truly going to make a difference in these statistics, I was going to have to reach every medium possible - not only through a book, but television, audio and videotapes, and the Internet. This required me to rethink what I was going to do. Where would I get the money for such a large project? Promoting the book would require me to be on TV and radio. Was I willing to put myself under the public eye? There was only one thing that could keep me from reaching this goal. *Me*! Was I willing to step up to be my best? The passion to make a difference drove me to say, "Go for it!"

I hope you enjoy and learn as much as I did from writing the book and having the opportunity to meet and interview these fabulous women. It was a great experience to meet other women who are life-long learners and willing to do what is necessary to be their best. They have learned to be very successful playing with the Big Boys and share great nuggets for success that anyone can learn from.

Chapter One

Leveling the Playing Field

Is your career important to you? Can you see where you are headed and exactly how to get there? What can you learn from others who have excelled? Whether you just want to further your career or go to the top, these Most Powerful Women (MPW) will show you the way.

This chapter highlights statistics about female officers in Fortune 500 companies, addresses why there are so few women in leadership positions, identifies the barriers to advancement, notes what women bring to the marketplace, and gives the shared success characteristics of these women. (If you want to compare how many of these 60 characteristics you possess, there's a checklist in the Actions and Attributes section in the back of the book.)

The Sad Statistics

The 1999 Catalyst's *Census of Women Corporate Officers and Top Earners*[2] reported that among Fortune 500 companies:

> • 11.9%, or 1,386, of the 11,681 corporate officers were women – compared to 88.1% men.

> • 5.1%, or 114, of the women out of 2,248 individuals hold the clout titles of Chairman, Vice Chairman, Chief Executive Officer (CEO), President, Chief Operating Officer (COO), Senior Executive Vice President (SEVP) or Executive Vice President (EVP). In other words, 94.9% of the positions of power and influence are controlled by men.

- 6.8%, or 375, of the total 5,525 line (profit-and-loss or revenue-generating) positions were held by women. These are the jobs that typically lead to the top officer position. Nearly half of all corporate officer positions are line officer jobs.

- Women earn 76% of what men do in comparable jobs.[3]

- 3.3%, or 77, of the 2,353 top wage earners (the five highest-paid in each firm) were women – compared to 96.7% men.

- 14.4%, or 72, of the companies currently have at least one woman among their five most highly paid officers – so 85.6% of the 500 companies lack a woman among their five highest-earning officers.

- 1.3%, or 105, women of color were officers in the 340 companies responding to the survey

- Based on an average rate of change since 1995, when corporate officer data was first gathered, women will occupy 13% of Fortune 500 corporate officer positions in the year 2000 and only 17% by the year 2005![4]

It took 70 years for women to win the right to vote. A large percentage of women now have been working full-time for over 30 years. Based on the current rate of change, it will take women another 45 years to reach parity in the executive ranks—just as long as it took to get equality at the polling booth! That is an incredible and unacceptable calculation. Because women made up 46.2%[5] of the workforce in 1998, shouldn't they have equal opportunities as corporate officers?

As we'll see, women's lack of prominence in upper echelons may be due in part to bias and institutional hurdles. But women are also restrained by how they view themselves. What will it take for women to exhibit more confidence in their abilities? The MPW can be role models and mentors for women who want independence, success, control over their own lives and are willing to take the action necessary.

The majority of female officers hold the traditional staff roles for women – Public Relations, Human Resources, and External Affairs. A large proportion of the 375 women officers in line positions are Chief Financial Officers. (CFO can be viewed as either a staff or line function.) That is not to say these are not important jobs. But the most powerful positions are those with profit-and-loss or revenue-generating responsibility (line positions). In addition, those are the jobs that typically lead to the top.

Shortly after Liz Fetter, currently President and CEO of NorthPoint Communications started working in Strategic Planning (a staff function) for Pacific Bell she was informed, *"I was told I needed to get a 'real' job. My first question was, what do you mean a real job? I was told it was something in Operations, where I'd learn how the company made money, a line function."*

Twenty-one percent, or 105, of the Fortune 500 companies have *no* women officers. Why would an ambitious, career-oriented woman work for a firm that lacks women officers when there are many companies supportive of women in management? (A section in the back of the book lists companies with a high percentage of women officers and the best and worst industries for women.)

Men have always had the power, status, and title, and continue to do so as shown by a closer look at some of the figures cited earlier:

- 88.1% of corporate officers are men
- 96.7% of the top wage-earning officers are men
- 94.9% of the clout titles are held by men
- 93.2% of the line positions are held by men

Why would the power structure want to change? A company does not change unless there is a reason. The biggest reason to change is that such a move is "good for business," that the company can increase its profits.

According to Faith Popcorn, a futurist who forecasts social, economic and political trends, women now have 60% of the buying power in this country.[6] What a contrast to their lack of clout in the business world!

Who knows how best to sell to women? *Women*! The fact that women have the purchasing power should move more of them into the executive ranks. If companies want to stay competitive, they will need to promote the best people for the job, regardless of gender.

Some women reach clout positions in companies, then realize they may never become CEO. They must then choose to stay and gamble their futures, or leave and go to smaller, even start-up, companies where they can run the firm in the way they believe best. But if women in high positions leave these large companies, who will be there to help other women reach the top and change existing policies?

Barriers to Advancement

Women face external as well as internal barriers. But the MPW you will meet in this book have learned to surmount both kinds. They realize that they will always have to overcome some type of adversity. In fact, some of these women state that even the *belief* in such barriers can be in the way of women's advancement. For example, Anne Sweeney, President of Disney/ABC Cable Network states, *"I've never been a proponent or a believer in the 'glass ceiling.' That kind of thinking has held more women back than helped them."* In other words, if the ceiling is what you focus on, that's what you will see.

Karen Garrison, President, Pitney Bowes Management

Services, prefers to talk about glass "walls" rather than ceilings. As she and Ursula Burns, Senior Vice President, Xerox, see it, false perceptions among their peers and subordinates about age, gender, and aggressiveness are much more troublesome than resistance from the top. However, as all the MPW agreed, if you feel top-level resistance and are sure you've done everything possible to win support, it is time to move on.

Keep an eye on the top executive. Typically, whatever the CEO believes and expects, management will, too. If the CEO doesn't want women on the leadership team, then there probably won't be any.

External barriers. As we've seen, most large businesses are controlled and run by men. Much of the leadership literature has traditionally focused on success traits drawn from male military or sports models. Most people achieve their greatest comfort level when surrounded by people who are like themselves. Thus, many men running businesses are most comfortable around other men. They may not be used to having women in decision-making positions, let alone the boardroom. A challenge they must deal with is getting past associating women in the office with their mother, girlfriend, spouse, ex-lover, aunt, or sister.

Men are also less likely to perceive hostility or exclusion in an environment designed by and for men. (Have you noticed that when men have a bad woman boss they may state, "I never want to work for a woman again?" But does anyone with a bad male boss say, "I never want to work for a man again!" Probably not.)

A Catalyst report[7] stated that most barriers for advancement are unintentional. "Rather, they are the consequence of unexamined assumptions about women's career interests and capabilities and unquestioned policies and practices that pervade the corporate culture."

In fact, male CEOs in another Catalyst survey[8] gave the following top reasons for why there aren't more women in high positions:

• Lack of experience –They thought it was riskier to place women in a line position then it was a man. Because the one who places the woman there is also taking a risk with his career, the tendency is to go the safer route. (But if women aren't given the opportunities in line jobs, how will they get the experience for higher positions?)

• Women have not been in the "pipeline" long enough to warrant consideration for senior-level positions. Corporate managers generally spend 25 years or more gaining experience for such jobs. (The issue shouldn't be how long someone is in the pipeline, but rather what they *did* while they were there?)

Viewing women as an integral part of their business and of the team is increasingly a necessity for any corporate leader's success. The women interviewed in this book have developed a style that men trust and are comfortable with.

These MPW also have learned to surround themselves not necessarily with people who are like them, but who are the *right* people: those with an attitude for success, team players who understand the vision, and bring different perspectives to the team. Without a variety of perspectives, issues can be viewed in a tunnel and opportunities missed.

Several of the MPW found in-house mentors who believed in them and were willing to risk placing them in line positions. Of course, the women *did* excel. It is through these women's examples that more women will be given opportunities.

In many ways, male senior officers who are not as supportive of women are merely mirroring the societal stereotypes. These stereotypes perceive women as less intelligent, holding lower positions and deserving of lower wages because they are not the traditional breadwinners. Women often are seen as less credible and not as employable as men. Women frequently need to work harder to be accepted, and even if they are accepted, some co-workers still will think the women should be home taking care of the children. Sometimes women are seen as undeserving of power and unlikely to know what to do with it even if they get it. Given such views in society at large, it's not surprising that many women have been programmed to fail because of the environment in which they were raised.

Among the other messages girls and women receive are that:

• It's better to seek security and dependence rather than to take risks and strive for control over their own destiny. Our soaring divorce rate suggests this perception is not realistic, yet it continues to prevail among many women.

• Smart, intelligent women intimidate many men. Because most people want to be in love and have a mate, this can keep women from fully utilizing their skills for fear of being alone.

• Women should take care of the household, no matter what. Men in the boardroom, typically, have wives at home who take care of everything for them. Luckily, many women have supportive mates that have allowed them to fulfill their dreams, including having a family.

• "Masculine" behavior traits in women sometimes are not welcome. Though each of us has a feminine and masculine side to our personalities, women who show more of their male side are sometimes criticized. One leadership research study[11] found that there were certain expectations that men will act in one way and women another. The masculine characteristics identified were tough, competent, direct, self-confident, possessing leadership, objective, aggressive,

forceful, and responsible. The feminine traits were
nurturing, compassionate, good communicator,
encouraging, sensitive, understanding, gullible, touchy
feely, and loyal. What's most important, though, is to use
the traits—whether masculine or feminine—that are
appropriate to the task.

Several MPW spoke of having to temper their
aggressiveness or enthusiasm. If the company views a woman's
aggressiveness as too "male" or her enthusiasm as too female, her
career could be hindered.

Jean Hamilton gives this advice: *"You have to be careful
about the way that you present yourself. But, it's rather nice to
have female and male sides and to have that show in the work
place. Simply put, just be yourself. I don't think there is an
inherent gender conflict in the workplace, especially if you remain
true to yourself, while acknowledging the environment that you're
operating in."* Both men and women need personality traits and
attributes, thinking patterns, and communications skills that cross
traditional gender boundaries.

The above perceptions do exist in our society today. The
MPW chose to overlook these and focus on what they wanted. By
doing so, all of their energies were used in an area that they could
control.

Internal barriers. These are the hurdles women create for
themselves because they may have been conditioned to think of
themselves in this way. The MPW show, these barriers, too, can be
overcome. It is all up to you on how you want to think and believe
in yourself.

Among the most common challenges of this sort are:

Not believing in your capabilities. All the MPW feel
competent to take on any assignment. That doesn't mean they
have the specific skills to do that job or know everything about it.

But they know they have the basic skills to do any task and can learn the specifics of a particular job. Do they ever question themselves? Sometimes, but their core belief in themselves is always there, and that confidence shows.

Not willing to do what is necessary to progress. Sacrifices will be necessary to move up the ladder. You may have to make a geographic move to get into the higher ranks. You may need to make tough choices about when you have children and how you will care for them. Men who have always been considered the breadwinners are often willing to leave a position and move on. Women tend to be more security oriented and will stay at a job longer than appropriate. Mary Farrell, Senior Investment Strategist at PaineWebber shares the impact of her choice, *"I won't leave my children for extended lengths of time and even my domestic travel is put into very small time frames so I will not be away from the kids for too long. It certainly hurt my career and I understand that and I accept that. I think it's fair. I didn't expect that I could announce I would not be competitive across the board and that it would be overlooked."*

Not understanding about playing on a team or figuring out the rules of the game. Business, like life, is a game. The question is how you choose to play it. Do you want to win, be your best, make a difference? Or, are you satisfied where you are? All games require mastering of the rules. All of the MPW are dedicated to life-long learning. They pay attention to what is happening around them. They find out what works and what doesn't. When something doesn't work they ask themselves *"Why?"* Then they take steps to correct their action or direction. They don't just say, "Oh, well, that didn't work."

Mary Farrell states, *"You really have to produce the performance; you have to be a team player and you have to be circumspect about understanding what the rules of the game are, so that you're playing by those rules. Women can have self-*

defeating behavior by refusing to understand the rules or to play by them."

Not being resilient. Boys are used to playing on teams and sometimes losing. So they play games to win, but when they lose they move on. This is good training for business. But some women have a tendency to see a loss as a personal blemish and then are reluctant to try again. Under this view, *they are a failure* rather than *they have failed*. The MPW, on the other hand, learned from their mistakes or failures and moved ahead.

Not promoting yourself. Women are taught as girls to be social, inclusive and not to brag about what they accomplish. They may not even be prepared to accept compliments. If someone says she did a great job, does the woman look the speaker in the eye and say, "Thank you"? Or, does she look away and lower her head? You may be working very hard, but if others don't know what you are doing and how it benefits the business, all that effort may never be recognized.

Too many people wait to be noticed. Jean Hamilton, CEO of Prudential Institutional, states, *"It's also important to talk about your accomplishments, not in a boastful fashion, but in a way which makes them clear. Some women have been a little less willing to promote themselves. There are a lot of decisions we all have to make every day about who should be promoted or who can do the job well. Obviously, the more that we know about an individual, the more likely we will be to consider them. I would advise women to make sure that, in the right way, their successes in the corporation are understood."*

Executives rely on their managers to provide the input about who are the top performers. Some managers aren't very good at doing this for themselves and therefore do not adequately represent their people. It is in your best interest to make the extra effort to seek out upper management and figure a way to subtly explain what you have contributed. Find a way that is comfortable for you to break the ice. Is it seeking out your bosses at a meeting? Asking about the team's results? Inquiring about the boss' family or personal life? Be prepared with what you are going to say. Do not attempt to wing this. You want to make the best possible impression.

The MPW have learned to overcome all of these interior barriers. If you possess any of these barriers, it can hold back your career.

What Can Firms Do?

Companies cannot be expected to change societal norms all by themselves. But right-minded organizations can do a lot to alter false perceptions about women. Programs can be put in place to advance women. For example, firms can:

> • Ensure equal numbers of men and women receive in-house leadership training.

> • Emphasize the recruitment of women.

> • Provide more flexible work policies—such as job sharing and flextime—that often appeal to women.

> • Designate high-potential employees, including women, and invest in their professional development.

> • Set up cross-functional job rotations.

The Strengths Women Bring

Businesses that make an effort to attract, retain, and promote women will find they bring incredible strengths to a rapidly-changing workplace. As Jean Hamilton states, *"The best management style is no longer 'command and control.' The ability to form strong groups and teams, to listen, and to delegate is becoming increasingly important in business today. I think women feel comfortable with this type of management style, which can give them a distinct advantage."*

The values that girls learn and the skills with which mothers raise their families can work very well in business. The ability to balance conflict, pace oneself, teach, guide, lead, monitor, network, and impart information are eminently transferable.

Specifically, women are generally given high marks for:

• **Being great multi-taskers.** Medical research has proven that women and men think differently. Men tend to be more linear thinkers (singular), whereas women have the ability to have more thought sequences going on at one time (multiple). Sometimes men take this women's way of thinking as being "flaky" or "scattered," but much of business involves tracking multiple projects and problems simultaneously.

• **Valuing relationships.** Women often place a high ethical value on cooperation and responsibility. While boys often are raised to fight for autonomy and reject intimacy, girls usually are encouraged to downplay conflict and seek consensus.

Karen Garrison states, *"You have to engage, not to be personal friends, not to be buddy buddies, but to know where people are on that gauge. Women do that better."* Ursula Burns emphasizes collaboration rather than competition, adding: *"From the beginning of time, we've been taught to nurture and work in groups. So there is this natural ability to include, even if there's difference, you include them, nurture, more than to compete"*

Women generally understand the importance of people skills and motivating employees. They are often great listeners and are willing to show they care. As Ellen Hancock, President and CEO, Exodus Communications, said, *"Caring is an important attribute that women can bring to this role as manager."*

• **Being intuitive**. Having intuition and knowing when to use it can be often applied in business. Rarely does a decision-maker have every possible fact. At some point, she has to rely on her own instincts. Ellen Hancock recalls a defining moment when she thought: *"'Wait a second, why am I waiting for all this input from all these people? I know the answer. I don't need that task force report. I know what the answer is here.' It definitely added to my value content in the equation. My instincts tell me, 'Let's go this way.' You become more of a leader when you do that, rather than just rubber-stamping someone else's report."*

Clearly, women are capable of holding *any* position within a company. If they work on the behaviors that hinder people's perceptions of them and persevere, they can achieve their career aspirations.

Shared Traits of the Most Powerful Women

In interviewing these women executives, I found many similarities among them. Their tone of voice and the way they carry themselves exudes confidence. All hard workers, they are constantly raising the bar for themselves and others in the organization. They have a sense that anything is possible. They believe that they can take themselves as far as their abilities will take them. For them, life is a self-fulfilling prophecy—if you can dream it you can do it. If you think you can or can't, you're right.

They all figured out how to adapt to organization's norms and pride themselves on being team players. Shelley Broader, Vice President at Hannaford Brothers, has coined a phrase that typifies how she (and the others) operate. *"I like people to develop with me and develop their own plans and I don't want to be incredibly directive in the way that I lead. I want to create followship."*

All the MPW committed themselves to working long hours early in their careers because they knew their priorities. In fact, perseverance and determination are part of their core being. They understand that they have to continually prove themselves. Still, they put organizational success before their own personal ambition. Driven to achieve, they constantly reassess their own skills and seek out what they need to learn. And they ask questions, lots of questions.

Most of the MPW were the first woman in their positions. So they learned to ignore unsupporting comments or perhaps deflect them with humor. If the comments became flagrant, though, they either spoke up about it or left. They are always true to their personal values--about who they are.

They create a vision within their organization and establish the strategy to accomplish the objective. They set strategies, develop action plans and set common goals with their teams. These women are organization builders, give ongoing feedback to their teams, and eliminate boundaries and turf battles. They use their power to achieve results and effect policies.

Their greatest challenge is balancing work and personal life. Family is number one for these women. For something important to their family, they are willing to stand firm by saying, "I won't do that because I have a family commitment." Several of the women stated that if the business is not willing to accept that, then you aren't working for the right company.

Yet they also realize that setting high goals means giving up something. As Ann Livermore, President at Hewlett-Packard, puts it: *"If you think about the top professionals in any field, they don't have balance. Think about an Olympic athlete. Would you call an Olympic athlete's life balanced? Or an actress? A business executive? No. It's hard to achieve balance."*

The next chapters are their success secrets in their own words. Listen and learn from the female Olympians of business.

"Another key to success is having the ability and willingness to open the door that someone else hasn't yet opened. Turn things upside down and think about them differently. Take things apart and put them back together again."

ANNE SWEENEY

- **President, Disney/ABC Cable Networks and President, Disney Channel**
- **Degrees: Bachelor of Arts – English**
  Master of Education
- **Children: 2**
- **Age: 41**

Anne Sweeney is responsible for non-sports cable programming for the Walt Disney Company and its ABC subsidiary. She oversees the operation of Disney Channel, Toon Disney and SoapNet as well as ABC's interest in Lifetime, A&E Television Network, the History Channel and E! Entertainment Television.

Interviewing Anne was a treat. She has a fresh perspective and believes in thinking outside of the box. She talks about anything being possible and the need to regularly ask yourself "Why not?"

You've had such an incredible career with the work you did at Nickelodeon and then launching FX (was a subsidiary of Fox) and now the fabulous work you've done at Disney. How have you done it?

"I've had a lot of fun and I've had a lot of help. The smartest thing I have done at all three companies was to build a very strong team of people--people who represented the absolute best in their individual departments and their individual disciplines. When you surround yourself with people who are smarter than you, the chance for success is much greater."

Where do you find those "right people"?

"You have to get out there. You have to do more than rely on the opinions of others. You have to join organizations. I belong to American Women in Radio and Television and Women in Cable and Telecommunications. These organizations have been responsible for introducing me to a lot of talented people."

Have you had to move out people who were not performing as well as the rest?

"It really starts with establishing a goal and working with your team to establish a goal and to very clearly articulate the mission and the vision of your business. Who are we and where are we going? I have found that just about ten times out of ten, the people who don't understand the mission and the vision and the people who can't grab onto the goal often take themselves out."

How did you get started at Nickelodeon?

"I had a very small beginning at Nickelodeon, but as I look back, it was quite a fateful day that took me to Nick. I had graduated from Harvard with a master's degree in education and was bound and determined to get a job in children's television. I had read about Nickelodeon while I was still in school. I moved from Cambridge back to the New York area and started doing my homework trying to find anyone who knew someone at Nickelodeon. This was the summer of 1980 and at that time Nickelodeon was very small. The channel was in approximately three million homes and had only ten employees. I remember contacting a former professor who put me in touch with Sandy Kavanaugh, who, at the time, was Nick's head of programming.

"I initially met with Sandy and was asked to come back in about a week. During my second meeting, I was interviewed simultaneously by three people--the head of development, the head of acquisitions and the head of production. Halfway through the interview one of the people asked me, "If you could pick one of our jobs to have, which one would you choose?" They weren't seriously giving me the option to choose. I said that the job in acquisitions sounded interesting to me, something I could do, and also something I had never done before; therefore, if given the opportunity to pick, probably the job in acquisitions would be the one for me.

"The manager of acquisitions at that time was Gerry Laybourne who later went on to become the head of Nickelodeon and has done marvelous things since. My career started about a month later, in January of 1981, as her assistant. I think I became the 11th person to work at Nickelodeon. The summer after I started, MTV was born and then we saw the creation of Nick at Night, the launches of VH-1 and a comedy channel called HA! which eventually, through a joint venture with HBO, came to be known as Comedy Central. It was a wonderful time to get started in the cable industry because I really got in on the ground floor. Ten, eleven people running the business, doing everything from on-air promotion to choosing all of the programming that we would buy, and creating all of the programming that we would produce ourselves."

When and why did you decide to move from Nickelodeon to FX?

"After 12 years at Nickelodeon, I was approached by Rupert Murdoch. I had recently completed negotiating a joint venture to launch Nickelodeon in the UK in partnership with his company, B Sky B. During this deal, I came to know many of the people at Sky. Rupert approached me and told me that he too was getting into the cable television business, starting a service which he described to me. He went on to offer me the job of CEO. I said, 'Well, thank you very much, but I'm not unhappy.' I went back to my boss at Nickelodeon, Gerry Laybourne, and told her. She said, 'Well, you just told me as your friend; when are going to tell me as your boss?' I thought about it for a moment and said, 'Well, Rupert Murdoch's just offered me a new job.'

"I spent the next four days making copious lists with my husband-- all the pros and cons of taking this job. It meant a move to California, uprooting our children, finding schools and housing, and creating a new life in a new place. My husband and I are both from

East Coast families, who never thought we would leave. In many ways it was the hardest week of my life because there were so many reasons to stay and so many reasons to go. I remember that Friday morning we woke up and my husband said, 'Well, life is an adventure. And if this is the adventure that you want to take, let's do it.'

"I recall thinking that was the worst thing that he had ever said to me. It would have been so much easier if he had said, 'No, we can't go.' That would have been something to either rebel against or something to accept, but he made it my decision. He had just completed law school. Mid-career, he decided to go back to school to become a lawyer. He graduated the night before I received the phone call from Rupert Murdoch."

Then it was an easy transition for him.

"Well, for him, it was a law firm on the East Coast or a law firm on the West Coast. He took both bar exams, just in case we didn't enjoy the adventure on the West Coast. I remember that Friday just really doing a lot of walking and thinking. It occurred to me that life really was an adventure and there was so much that I didn't know and so much that I'd be tested on and that's actually what was so attractive to me. I told Gerry about my decision. Then I called Rupert, and being the fast moving person that he is, he had a contract over to me for a signature that evening. A week later, I arrived in California."

Did you experience fear in making this huge decision?

"Curiously, no. I knew that my family was comfortable with it, and though our extended family was not happy about the move, they were committed to visit us. I really felt that if I didn't do it, I would never know, and I hate not knowing! I hate those unanswered questions. I was very uncomfortable with the thought of living the rest of my life not knowing if I could start a business from scratch, if I could ever live in another city in another state, if I could just start all over again. What I always loved about Nickelodeon was the fact that we had to make the rules up as we went along. We had to create something out of nothing. This was all so new, undiscovered and unknown to an extent. I grew up with three networks and PBS. On a good day, you could get some of the local stations from Schenectady, Albany and Troy--that was a big deal in television. I really loved the adventure of it and that kind of blocked out any fear. You don't have time to be fearful when you're trying to figure it out."

Do you think part of your big drive was the challenge, the unknown, what's over the hill?

"Exactly. What is on the other side of that? What if I decide that we can do it differently? I only hired courageous people who could say 'why not?' We all knew coming in that it was going to be hard, that it was going to be so different from anything we had ever done before. A day didn't pass that you didn't have a stack of unanswered questions and the next day, you had to invent new ways of answering those questions.

"It is that thrill that gets you out of bed. My experience at FX was a marvelous adventure. Gerry had finished at Nickelodeon and was being courted by Disney. She asked me if I would be interested in coming to run Disney Channel. The opportunity made me realize that as much as I had loved my three years at Fox, I had really missed being in the "kids" business and I had also never done family television. So now, I had a new adventure to consider, but more importantly, the chance to do something else I hadn't previously done. I remember a very dear friend of mine saying to me, 'This family thing, it's never going to work. And everyone will forgive you if you fail because no one has ever done it.' I just thought, 'Boy, those are fighting words,' and that we should be able to figure out the key to programming for families.

"There is excitement in the on-going challenge for the Disney brand. Probably the most wonderful thing I've learned here is that we can actually create the new definition of family. As my mother always put it, a family is wherever there is love."

Nickelodeon and Fox were start-ups for you. When you came to Disney you were then working in a big corporation. Did that change your perspective of the business or how you functioned in that environment?

"I feel that the start-up mentality is critical to success. It is very important to look at things as if they are brand new. When I joined Disney Channel in 1996, it was 13 years old and had been created in 1983 as a pay-service.

"I remember when Disney Channel launched because I was the person at Nickelodeon who taped it and then brought the tapes into the office. We were very, very threatened by Disney getting into the cable business. However, since Nickelodeon was basic service and Disney Channel was a pay service, their paths really didn't cross that much. When I arrived at Disney, the channel had started to transition to basic service and was in 10 million basic cable homes and four million pay homes. Today, Disney channel is in 64 million homes--one million pay and 63 million basic.

"I inherited a very smart distribution strategy and a very talented team. We just put more lighter fuel on the grill basically and really went to town. Another thing that we did which was really critical concerned the channel's programming. When I first came onboard, Disney Channel was being programmed as a pay television service.

I felt that it was essential that the programming mirror the sales strategy. The job really became how do you take the Disney brand into this new scenario. The Disney brand is known for its movies. The Disney brand is known for its animation. How does that now translate to the world of basic cable? We had some wonderful programming and creative issues to take on."

What else is part of your success formula?

"It is important to always find the unknown exciting. Another key to success is having the ability and willingness to open the door that someone else hasn't yet opened. Forge the new path. Turn things upside down and think about them differently. Take things apart and put them back together again. Everything is up for grabs."

Were there any particular events in your life that prepared you to hold such a leadership position?

"In many ways, it is all about the way I was raised.

"My mother is a retired elementary school teacher and my father is a retired elementary school principal. I grew up believing we ran the school business. I was set-up early on by my parents to be a life-long learner. Teachers were there to excite you about information and opportunity but it was up to you to do the learning, to take it to the next level. I grew up with parents who said, 'Be whatever it is you want to be.'

"When I went to college I had every intention of becoming a teacher. I took a child psychology course my freshman year. As part of the course, I was required to go to the campus preschool and work with little kids a couple of days a week. After several weeks of this, I called my mother and said, 'I don't know how you do this. This is so hard. I can't be responsible for teaching kids how to read and write.' My mother said, 'Thank God you found out now.' I was expecting, and I don't know why because they never said it, but I was expecting, 'Well, you better get your head around this.'

"Her response was very freeing. It was not unlike my husband's 'life is an adventure' line. In essence, my parents were saying the same thing: figure out what it is that makes you tick. I came out of the experience knowing I wanted to do something for kids, I just didn't know what it was.

"In my senior year of college, I had an internship at Children's Television Workshop and I worked on Sesame Street and the Electric Company magazines. The job was testing early iterations of the magazines with little kids and finding out what worked and what didn't work. Earlier that same year I became a page at ABC and was exposed to another side of the TV business--the very unglamorous side of television where you open the door for people, help audience members to their seats, or escort guests to the green room or the make-up room. It was really those two factors that made me decide to go into children's television."

What was your greatest success?

"My kids, my kids, my kids. . . . If I'm not a successful parent, then nothing else really matters."

How did you change along the way, as you were working up from that assistant or page position to where you are now?

"I had to become a better listener. I had to listen more carefully to everything from people's advice to how they did their jobs. I found out that the more carefully I listened, the better idea I had about the path I wanted to take. That's really what made all the difference."

Anything else you can think of?

"Beyond listening, I'd say doing. The risk-taking, and trying things.

"I remember my mother saying (about Nickelodeon), 'What is it again? We don't get it on our television set. Is it advertising for kids?' The idea of a television network delivered by cable for kids was brand new. It was very foreign. The idea of music videos on television was very foreign. The idea of 24-hour news. All of the things that we take for granted today.

"I remember a lot of my friends going to work for Xerox. Xerox came to campus to recruit, as did IBM, companies that were recognized. Cable television definitely fell into the category of, 'What was that again?'"

How did you feel when your friends were going off to the big ten and you were going to this small start-up, even though it was under a large umbrella?

"I loved it because I felt enormous freedom. I've always felt that I've done my best when I had a lot of room. I've done my best when there weren't a lot of rules, when there was something to be fixed or something to be created."

What were some of your other key learnings?

"One of the key learnings that came a little bit later in life was the balance issue.

"In my early days at Nickelodeon I was at my desk easily between

7:00 and 8:00 a.m. The staff was very young; I think the average age in the company was 24 when I joined, and it was a really fun group of people. We were all starting out and we were all building something from nothing. We were probably fairly alike because we had jumped into this great unknown and we would work until 8:00 at night, and then all go out for dinner together or to a club or to do something. Those early years in New York, at Nickelodeon, I remember so fondly. We were in it for the adventure and we were there on the ground floor. As a result, many of us have gone on to run cable networks and other kinds of businesses because we had an experience that couldn't be replicated anyplace else. All because we took a chance.

"Early on, it was fine to work the 12-18 hour days, but I was married in my mid-20's and started to have my children in my late 20's, early 30's. There came a point when putting in 18 hours a day at the office was no longer possible. I think the greatest struggle I've had, probably since the day my oldest child was born, has been finding the balance between life and work. And really making sure that both sides are healthy and both sides get what they need from me."

Is it figuring out what that health is, and when the health is not there, putting more attention toward it?

"That is certainly part of it. I try not to judge myself too harshly. I constantly evaluate how I spend my time--what is productive and what is not.

"My daughter is actually a perfect illustration. When I arrived at Disney we were doing focus groups with kids and the parents separately to get a handle on what was going on in kids' lives and in families' lives. During these groups, we heard more than once, in more than one city across the U.S., kids use the term 'quality time.'

The first time I heard it, I thought, 'Oh, somebody is talking in the car pool. This is definitely an adult term. We don't know where this kid picked it up.' Well, we heard it in New York, in Atlanta, in Chicago, and in Houston. I started to think, 'Maybe there's something to this.'

"I was driving somewhere with my daughter and I asked her what she thought quality time was. As an adult, I thought that perhaps she needed a little bit of help, so I prompted her: 'Is it going on vacation, is it going to a movie?' She said, 'Mom, Mom, you don't get it. It's not the big stuff, it's anything we do together.' At that point, I realized that you have to give the same weight to going to the grocery store with your children as you would to taking them to the big hit movie that they've been dying to see or to that big vacation that you've planned forever. In their minds, those 'big' things are just as important as staying home and watching a movie on TV on a Saturday night.

"It's about being with them. It's not necessarily what you do when you're with them, just that you're with them--that you're snuggled up next to them on the couch. Even that time in the car is precious. Turn off the radio; you don't need those tapes. Have the conversation. Use those minutes to talk about what happened in school, or talk about something you read or a book that they're reading. Engage them."

What have been defining moments for you?

"Gee, there have been so many. Certainly when my kids were born were defining moments. It's interesting, the defining moments before they were born were probably pretty standard--graduating, my first job, getting married. But when my children were born, suddenly the defining moments changed and my defining moments now are really intertwined with theirs.

"It's everything from the first time my son spoke to taking my daughter to her first day of kindergarten. Watching her go to kindergarten was just fascinating. This moment of watching the independence of a five-year-old blew me away probably as much as Murdoch saying, 'I want you to come and start my cable networks for me.' It was something I brought into the office that day.

"In Los Angeles, everyone kind of knows where everybody works, especially if you're at a studio. My daughter's kindergarten teacher said to her, 'I hear your mommy has a new job.' She looked up at her teacher with all the pride in the world, she said, "Yes, my mom's the president of Disneyland.' And that for her was it. That's what Disney was. Disney Channel wasn't part of her viewing experience but boy, Disneyland summed up Disney for her."

What were the "unwritten rules" you uncovered as you were going through your career?

"Oh, I always think that when you start at a company there's always someone or several people who will tell you that's not the way we do it. Rule number one in a new job is there are no rules, and we start from scratch. I've never been a proponent of or a believer in the 'glass ceiling.' That kind of thinking has held more women back than helped them."

Anything else, other than that there are no rules?

"Yes, you just decide that you're going to. You're going to do what is necessary. When you identify that goal and that vision, that alone should make you unstoppable."

Is there anything else you'd like to add?

"Never choose the safest route simply because it is the safest route. I believe that if you stay in jobs where you know you cannot fail, you will never grow. Along the way, you must be prepared to take risks and make mistakes. I mean *big* mistakes. Mistakes that people know about. Mistakes that people may even write about. Mistakes that will make you question whether you have in fact chosen the right path. This sort of risk-taking constitutes an act of faith in yourself. You are saying to yourself, 'It will not be easy, but I am willing to accept this challenge.' Once you make that leap and establish that kind of faith in yourself, you will be able to find it in others and to help instill it in others."

"There are so many things that you can work on, so many things that you can do in a business environment, but picking the right ones and letting other people handle the rest is a really important lesson."

ANN LIVERMORE

- **President, Business Customer Organization at Hewlett-Packard Member of Hewlett-Packard's Executive Council**
- **Degrees: Bachelor's degree – Economics Master of Business Administration**
- **Children: 1**
- **Age: 41**

As president of Hewlett-Packard's Business Customer Organization, Ann Livermore is responsible for helping customers reinvent their businesses so they can gain competitive advantage in the Internet economy. Her team creates powerful solutions that fully exploit HP's assets in information appliances, e-services, and always-on Internet infrastructure to transform the customer experience across entire industries. Fortune Magazine named Livermore the 13th most powerful woman in business in 1999.

Ann learned early in life how important it is to push yourself past your own perceived limits. It is only through doing that you grow and continue to learn.

How did you get started at HP?

"I entered HP directly from Stanford, where I had been at graduate school. The man who interviewed me grew up in Greensboro, the same little town where I grew up in North Carolina. It was almost like fate."

You probably never thought that you would be there this long.

"No, in fact, when I went to HP, I thought I would stay a year or two and then leave. I really thought that HP would be a great company for me to get some business training. I always envisioned that I would go to HP for a couple of years, and then leave and go to a small company. But I didn't."

Did you find there was a time in your career when you thought, "I have to make a decision. Am I going to stay here or am I going to go someplace else?"

"A couple of years after my daughter was born, we thought about moving back to North Carolina to be close to my family. That had more to do with the family tugs that you have. My husband and I thought about that for a year or so, and then decided to stay in the San Francisco bay area. I've never really gotten the itch to leave since I've been at HP."

What is success to you?

"Success for me is doing the very best job that I can--having a goal laid out and then having me or my team be able to achieve that goal.

"Success is really important in my personal life, in sports, and in business. I measure success in a lot of dimensions, other than solely what I do in my business life at HP."

What type of dimensions?

"It's really important to me to have success in my family life: to have my family happy with what I'm doing, with what they're doing, and with what our life's like. There are successes around little things: games, growing a plant, working in the garden. Lots of things can create success."

Do you write your goals down?

"No. My goal is always, in whatever I'm doing, to do the best that I can and to achieve a successful outcome. I've been lucky, because Hewlett-Packard is a company that rewards results. When you achieve good business results, it doesn't matter if you're a man or a woman, or what you look like. What matters is that you've laid out a business objective and achieved the results. That is the thing that has helped me to able to be successful at HP--I'm results-oriented."

How have you had to change, as you were going up the corporate

ladder to be successful?

"I had a very thoughtful, very helpful boss--a man named Jim Arthur. One of the things that Jim said to me was, 'Ann, you care about too many things!' It was a really important message because there are so many things that you can work on, so many things that you can do in a business environment, but picking the right ones and letting other people handle the rest is a really important lesson. That was hard for me. Choosing the ones that are really going to have an impact on our customers or our business is an important skill."

How did you learn to let go?

"It was a sheer matter of time. Jim used to tease me, 'It's not my fault if you can't get your job done in a regular work week.' I'd be working really late or working hard over the weekends. It forces you to prioritize things and pick those items that are going to have the biggest impact on the business results."

Were there any events as you were growing up that prepared you to hold such a leadership position?

"The thing that probably had the biggest impact on me is that I grew up with a mother and father who instilled in me the desire to be fair, but also the desire to play hard and to always do the best that I could. That nurturing and training as I grew up was a really important factor for me because it had a huge impact on the way I approach my job. The day-to-day things as I grew up reinforced those values and those ethics."

Did you have any role models when you were growing up? What did you learn from them?

"I had several role models of different types. Clearly, my mother was one of my most powerful role models. The biggest compliment that my father ever paid me was saying that I was the 1990's version of my mother.

"She worked on a lot of volunteer activities, and was quite powerful because she was getting people to do things who weren't getting paid for it. Some of the strongest leaders are people who do things in volunteer areas, because they're leading a group of volunteers who are there for the love or interest of it, as opposed to being driven by a business objective."

What have been your biggest learning lessons?

"The biggest learning lessons for me tend to come from interacting with people and learning how to get people to get things done. It's the very simple lesson of realizing how powerful it is just to recognize someone, to thank them for what they've done, to motivate them to do that much more. Reward and recognition can inspire great behavior, great results.

"Different people like to be recognized in different ways. But I can't think of anybody I have interacted with who hasn't appreciated being recognized for a job well done. Even something as basic as sending them a note, or telling them, 'You did a super job on that!' It's a very powerful motivator and yet so simple.

"One of the lessons I've learned is that in business, when things are going well, that's when you want to be toughest. When things are going well, people can take it. You want to push to go the extra mile and to extend your lead that much further. When things are shaky, that's when my team needs me to be more like a rock, to be solid, to be encouraging, to be motivating. Different people have different styles, but I tend to be toughest when things are good and most supportive when things are bad."

What is your greatest success?

"My greatest success came when I was about 18 years old and I went to a place called the National Outdoor Leadership School. It's a lot like Outward Bound. At the point I went to this program, I had never slept outside in a tent. I was not a hiker, a climber, or a water crosser. This was a program that I participated in as part of the University of North Carolina, and my greatest accomplishment was living through it.

"It was very far out of my norm, and I knew absolutely nothing. I was starting at as raw a base point as I possibly could. I learned that I could push myself beyond any limits I ever dreamed of."

Did you have role models there or was it a case of just getting through it?

"It was a case of getting through it, but also there were role models for me there--people who had a lot of experience and were eager to see me be able to do it and do it really well. I learned that sometimes you have to depend on other people. That was not something I was used to. I was used to plowing my way through and getting things done on my own. Suddenly, I had to depend on a whole group of people I didn't know very well to be able to make things happen."

Have you had mentors in your career? Where did you find them, and what did they do for you?

"I've had a couple of mentors. I can't say that I knew at the time that they were mentors. One of them was a person I worked with. Mark could make me so angry--mentoring was not necessarily a pleasant experience with him, but he pushed me and he knew things that were really important about business. He knew how to make money. He knew how to make customers happy. He was very good at making people focus on the key things. He could really push people, but I really loved it."

Many times managers don't like to take a tough position, like giving negative feedback. Yet, that is what enables people to grow.

"Absolutely. That and really pushing you to your limits. It's back to the same thing that I learned out in the wilderness. You think *this* is your limit and then suddenly you get pushed to *there,* and that's what growing is all about."

What types of "unwritten rules" have you uncovered that have led to your success?

"The unwritten rules at HP are about how you get things done. A lot of it has to do with gaining support for an idea--where are the points of resistance going to be, and how do you work through building the support to make something big and powerful happen. A lot of that's not written. It's not a process laid out in which you talk to 'Joe,' then you talk to 'Susie,' then you talk to 'Pete,' and then it's over. That's just not the way things happen. Really understanding how to make the company work is one of the more fascinating sets of unwritten rules at most large companies."

Can you think of any other unwritten rules, other than learning how to get support for projects?

"How to communicate to a wide, dispersed field organization. I have responsibility at HP for all of our sales reps, services, and support people, and they're all over the world. Leading a distributed team is a lot different than leading a focused team that's in one geographic area. The importance of communication, the importance of having clear, consistent goals are very basic things and yet they're hard to do."

In a book I read[14], CEOs of large companies were interviewed from all over the world, and there are still some thoughts that women should remain at home. I'm thinking, "What year are we in?"

"Yes, even inside the United States there are corporations where there aren't very many women in the work force. Part of what happens is that some of the men are not used to interacting with women in the business environment. They're used to women in the role of a daughter, a wife, or a neighbor, as opposed to a business colleague. It is something that you learn."

There are such a small number of women in leadership positions in Fortune 500 companies. What do you think is the reason for that?

"Part of it has to do with the environment and part of it has to do with choices that people make. It's a big choice to decide that you want to be a top executive at a Fortune 500 company. You're making a commitment. How many women are in a position where they choose to make that commitment? Companies work as a kind of organism, and the organism keeps going the same way it always has unless there's a reason to change. You can look at all sorts of vectors of diversity, and some companies just aren't very diverse; they tend to be more comfortable promoting and hiring people who look and think the same way as all the previous officers did."

Balance is important, and you have a ten-year-old. What decisions or choices do you make that allow you to bring balance into your life?

"I don't believe in balance. I've decided that for me, balance is an unachievable objective. What I'm after is not work/life balance. What I'm after instead of balance is doing a great job in my work life and having a very happy home life. My family has to love what I do.

"If you think about the top professionals in any field, they don't have balance. Think about an Olympic athlete. Would you call an Olympic athlete's life balanced? Or an actress's? A business executive's? No. It's hard to achieve balance."

What has been your biggest challenge?

"My biggest challenge is carving out enough time for myself. I find that I'm at my best when I can have a sliver of time that's just for me--not for my family, not for my friends, not for my job, but just for me. Having that sliver of time helps reinvigorate me."

When you get that slice of time, what do you like to do?

"I read novels. I hit some golf balls. I putter around outside in the yard."

Is there any one particular thing you would say about your style, about who you are or how you do things, that has enabled you to be so successful?

"I'm fair and even-tempered. I can take a volatile situation and help get it to a point of resolution. That's one of my strengths. I'm also good at clearly laying out the most critical factors that need to be achieved to reach a certain business result."

We all have to make sacrifices in our lives. What sacrifices do you make, other than your personal time?

"Most of the sacrifices have to do with how I choose to spend my time. I don't have very much spare time, and I do a lot of multitasking."

Is there anything that you regret?

"I would have liked to have lived overseas at some point in my life. That would be hard to do now. But if I were doing it all over, I would have tried to have an overseas assignment at some point. Now I spend probably half my time overseas anyway. It would have been exciting to have actually lived in a different country and experienced it at a personal level, not just at a business level."

What have been the defining moment or moments in your life?

"There have been a number of defining moments in my life. The one that was the most emotional, the most touching, was when my mother died. One of the things that it taught me is the importance of enjoying every moment of life and never taking things for granted. So often you don't realize how much impact either family members or friends have had on you until you don't have them anymore."

In several magazine articles about powerful women, these women stated that they didn't feel powerful. How do you deal with the power that comes with your position?

"Power comes with the position. I feel it the most when I'm in front of or with a large group of my employees. For me, the power comes from realizing just how many people's lives I'm impacting, how many people I'm leading. Am I leading them to a good place? Am I making a good thing happen for them? I have become aware of the power that I have. But day-to-day, I don't really think about it. There are defining moments when it really hits.

"When you're a leader, you're always being watched, and people take everything that you do as a signal. Is she smiling today, is she frowning today? What was the tone of her voice? Do you think that twitch meant something? When you're a leader, people are watching you all the time."

How did you get used to people watching you all the time?

"It really does make you tune up a little bit. There's a performance aspect to being a leader. Your troops want to see a performance that exudes confidence. That's important. Yet, on the other hand, people also want to see that you have a heart."

How do you show that?

"Through showing emotion, and through showing passion and commitment for what you're doing. People really like to see the human side of leaders. It's important for leaders to find the right balance between being strong and analytical, and showing some emotion."

Would you do anything differently?

"Looking back on my life, I don't have any regrets. I feel incredibly lucky."

"Your employees get you promoted; your peers allow you to be promoted."

ELLEN HANCOCK

- **Chairman and Chief Executive Officer, Exodus Communications**
- **Degree: Bachelor of Science--Mathematics**
              Master of Science--Mathematics
- **Children: None**
- **Age: 56**

Ellen Hancock was the first woman senior vice president at IBM, National Semiconductor, and the chief technology officer at Apple Computer before moving to Exodus Communications and taking the company public.

The pivotal point in Ellen's career was when she was asked to move to North Carolina and become a manager. She had to make a decision about her career, her relationship with her husband, her family, and where she was willing to live.

What is success to you?

"Well, it varies. It's an achievement of a goal. That goal could be as simple as getting a product to market, having a very successful business, or becoming the chief executive officer of a public company. I've been fortunate in being able to accomplish many of those goals. Success responds to your own intentions and what you aspire to do."

What would you consider to be your greatest success?

"I tend to list successes in terms of business accomplishments-- they each have their own flavor. Being able to be named senior vice president of IBM and being the first female to have achieved that particular role and position certainly was, for me, an awesome event. But I've also said that I really did want to become CEO of a public company, and I've got to list that as one that's been very important to me. One is based with 29 years with a company and the other is based on a year and a half. They have slightly different perspectives."

What were defining moments in your life that were turning points in your career?

"There were several. One is that I did have people at IBM, executives at IBM, who decided to mentor me and give me advice on my career. I believe the decision to go from being a technical employee, one who worked on her own, to agreeing to go into the management ranks, for me was a defining moment. I had to agree to take on the role of leadership and the role of management and do both the pleasant roles that management includes and the very difficult ones. It took me awhile to make that decision, to agree to do that, and then as soon as I did, IBM supported me in that view.

"I spent a fair amount of time in the software side of the business and one of my mentors convinced me that I really needed to spend some time on the hardware side, which involved a physical move down to Charlotte, North Carolina. That too, has given me a background that has been very helpful in a lot of other jobs.

"Each time you make a decision on a career path change, it builds a portfolio, a skill base. I did agree when I was leaving North Carolina to take a role that I was excited about, but it was a staff position. But it gave me a tremendous view into the company, and then allowed me to leave that staff position and go back into a line position, and eventually become a division president and then a group executive with several divisions. What was helpful about all those changes is that when I did get the promotions, the promotions were leading some place.

"I've a strong view that when you look at a particular job change, or these defining moments, that you really should assess whether that change leads to the next one and whether you like where that goes. I've advised people, and follow this myself, to look two steps out, and if you like where that is and you like where that's headed, then this next step is the right step. That particular path has been very good to me. I always said that I would take roles that lead me towards a CEO position. I would hope not to take roles that would side-path me from that particular position. That's worked well for me."

What issues did you have to deal with in making the decision to move to North Carolina, and how did it affect your family?

"Some of it was very personal, and my husband and I had just put a down payment on a new kitchen in our house in Connecticut and I thought that was important. The executive who was trying to convince me to take this job was not at all interested in my kitchen. We agreed that I would consider the job. Then my husband considered some jobs in Charlotte and was concerned about his own role relative to that transition. He asked how long I was going to stay in Charlotte. I said, 'It's probably two years, maybe three.' He said, 'You know, we're going to be doing this again.' I said that I thought so. He said, 'Well, look Ellen I don't really mind being a supportive husband, but I don't want to be a camp follower, so I'll see you when you get back from Charlotte.' That played very well for us. We've done follow-up moves the same way. It's allowed each of us to make decisions about our careers, and yet still have this cross-country marriage. Charlotte taught us a lot.

"I also had moved, in IBM parlance, from being a first-line manager, where I had employees working for me, and went directly into a third line, skipping the second line. It allowed an escalation of my career, if you like. It took me from running a small group to a much larger group of employees."

When you made that decision, did you have any idea of the impact it was going to have?

"I could tell from the way that the company was describing it, when they said, 'We'd like you to consider this job.' There's another way, where they can say, 'We have this opportunity for you.' It's when they use that second sentence that you say, 'The company has decided.' You are either going on with the recommendation of your firm or you're blocking their recommendations. It was clear to me that a lot of thought had been given to that job, that there was an agreement within the company that that was the right job for me. Considering how careful IBM is about career management, I would essentially be running against what was the common wisdom in the firm. I knew it was an important step. But it was my acknowledging that my career was important and that I would agree to make some sacrifices--and it was clear it was not something I had been planning but that a career in IBM was important to me. It was a demonstration for both of us, for the company and myself, and also for my spouse to say, 'Yes, this is important for all three of us.'"

Some people feel that if they say "no" this time, they won't be asked again.

"It's a legitimate concern. It's not always followed up and practiced. I have been involved in several situations where the executive team feels an employee or a manager is extremely good. We try once or twice on a particular move--that move doesn't take place for whatever reason and you go back a third time; there will eventually be an end to that--but you will go back a third time for an employee or an executive that is worth it. I wouldn't say the first refusal is terminal--though it's not career enhancing--but you can, over time, bypass it. It's not as important. It's just that you have taken a first pass indicating that you are placing some other things, perhaps, above that particular career. In some cases, that is the right answer."

You've allowed some people to work for you for six months, including traveling and attending meetings with you, to see if they really wanted your type of position.

"I thought this was an excellent way to get an early sense of whether people continued to think this looked good to them or if they were horrified by how invasive it is, how much time you're really spending, how much it interferes with your personal life. If they felt that it was still something they wanted, because the job looked good, you'd say, okay, let's work on that next step. It was a good experiment in terms of whether the person really liked the role once it was understood what the role really meant. It's easy to say, 'I'd like to be president of a division.' It's another thing entirely to watch how the president of the division has to travel, work and the like. It's a good experience."

What about having a balanced life?

"I would describe it as being successful, but not balanced. Women who take these particular roles--and for whatever reason, I think this more true of women than perhaps men--are still obligated or feel obligated to work harder than many of our peers who are male. There are sacrifices. But, your friends and family, your spouse, your parents, all do have to support the situation and have an understanding that yes, this is important and so are friends and family. Your schedule probably does not allow you to perhaps be as available as some other people in that same family might be able to be."

It's said that we learn from our failures. At one point when you were responsible for IBM's networking hardware, your team stood behind the IBM technology and did not see where the competition and market were going. What did you learn from this?

"You have to be very focused. You need to know where your core competencies are, but you always have to watch that next space (the future) so you understand where that next space is going.

"I learned not to stay in my comfort zone, and to always watch around me, to see what is changing next. Do I have to change again just to respond to something new that wasn't there six months ago when I established a strategy? I also believe in execution. You can spend all your time on strategy and forget the fact that you were supposed to have executed. I tend to be someone who focuses a lot on execution.

"I take responsibility for what happened. I'll make other mistakes."

Could you comment on the "glass ceiling"?

"It's clear that there are glass ceilings. My advice to women is if they're working in a company that's not supportive, leave! There are a lot of other companies that are supportive. It makes no sense for women to try to think they're going to change the company they're in. That does not work. Wait until you can run a company and then you can change it."

There are influencing skills required in any position. What type of influencing skills have you used?

"There are some that come naturally to a person. You have to know which ones are natural to you and which ones need some fortification. It is not natural for me to discuss my salary with people and I knew I needed some assistance on that.

"In terms of convincing employees, again it depends on how important the subject is. If the subject is business related, you can often do that in a business environment. If the subject is more personal, like should you really move from Raleigh to New York, I've found that can be done much better over dinner-- some little bit of quiet, casual time where you can talk person-to-person and not within the confines of your calendar that allows you an hour for this conversation.

"It is important to ask yourself how serious the negotiation is. Is it something that fits within an hour--do I have my five charts that are compelling, and therefore, I know I'm going to walk away from this discussion very well placed--or is it tricky? If, for example, it's a contentious issue, then I'd strongly recommend that you spend a little bit of time going through and up the company and building up your support, so that there are other executives who support what you're trying to do."

How did you acquire your communication, leadership and influencing styles?

"I would say that most of this was on-the-job training. I did attend some classes. But more of it was essentially, over time, building up my style, and in fact understanding for myself what my style is. I remember fairly early in my career as a manager, I had about 200 people, and I sent a note off to one of the executives working for me. I had read a letter and didn't understand all the terms in the letter. I still remember saying; 'Do you understand what this term means?' He sent a note back and said, 'Why do you think you need to know it? Ellen, you're spending all your time in details. You're doing my job, his job, and everybody else's job. We need you to raise yourself a little bit above that.' I thought that was a good lesson.

"I asked some people if they thought I was into too many details. The answer was, 'Yes, Ellen, you don't need to get that deep into it. You need to know enough so that you're comfortable presenting what we do, but you don't need to know as much as we do.' I learned a little bit about delegation. Now, you have to know someone pretty well to get into this kind of dialogue.

"Trust is an important part of my scheme. If I trust people, I expect them to trust me. But I have to say that I've built up a style; I now understand what my style is. I know when it works and I know when it doesn't work as well. But it's worked well enough for me that I'm holding onto it. It took a while, with people essentially helping me, to understand when I was most able to get their support, and when I made it a little bit more difficult for myself than perhaps I should have."

We all have moments where we have received great advice or help from others. What is one of yours?

"I would say I got help from the people working with me and also from mentors. In one of my first jobs, again down in Charlotte, the executive who asked me to go down there, or encouraged me to go down there, would come down and visit. I remember one visit. IBM has this program where they ask the employees how the manager is doing. I had 50 people, and he asked, 'How do you think you're going to do on the survey?' I said that I hoped I would do well. He said, 'I don't know what you mean by 'hope.' Aren't you working on it? Aren't you making sure that your employees think you're a good manager?' I thought I was. He said, 'Look, Ellen, you may be very good. You may be excellent, as a person. You may be very bright as an individual. You may be hard working. But that will not lead you to success at IBM. It will not lead to executive positions, because you will be successful in a company like IBM only if your employees want you to get promoted.'

"I went back there and said, 'Oh, these employees are in charge of my career!' It does put a slightly different spin on it. That's another management lesson. That's what management is. I don't think you're born a great manager. I was terrified of becoming a manager, but you learn to become a manager. That's why I said it's on-the-job training when you pick up some of these things, such as the fact that your employees get you promoted, your peers allow you to be promoted. I mean that in a very strong sense, that you get promoted again when your peers think you're doing well and when they think you're a part of their team. And then, of course, if you're responding to what your management thought. It's very important that you take that full circle and that you look at all three constituencies and say, 'Am I responsible?' That's when some of the people working for me have said, 'You know, Ellen, you have developed a style and it's almost a mothering style. We can tell you care not just about how we're doing in this particular job, but we get a sense you care about our career.' Some of them have said, 'You're the first manager I've ever had who worried about *my* career, and me as a person.' That becomes part of your own style system."

When I was managing people I would ask them, "Where do you want to go?" Many times they had no idea about what they wanted to do in the future.

"Sometimes they're thrown when you say, 'I don't think you should be working for me any more.' And the response is, 'Why not?' The answer is, 'You need a broader sponsorship. You also need a skill base in a group that's different from the one I'm managing.' Once they understand you really are doing it from their perspective, you have their career in mind, and you force them to focus on the fact that they *have* a career, it builds a bond. Many times what would happen is the person would go off and take another job and then later, I'd be able to hire them and they were obviously a much better executive by then.

"It's a great circle. People laugh and say, 'Ellen has either put people in other organizations, so she has her friends covering her in other places, or she's just getting ready to bring them back home again.'

"Once you've realized it that way, then it's more in line with caring. That is an important attribute that women can bring to this role as manager."

How do you communicate that caring?

"I happen to be a private person, and you have to get a little more open about saying, 'I really care for you,' or periodically remembering to thank people who have done something exceptional. Or just spending some personal time with them--that personal aspect. I've had people working in other countries who I would trust with my life. I just know that if anything's happening, they will tell me; I will hear about it. They are my protectors in another part of the geography. It's very hard to build an organization where you don't have that kind of trust. It's important for them to know that you have it. And then they respond in kind. I cannot tolerate lack of integrity, and trust and loyalty. If you don't think those two things are key, somebody else is probably a better boss. I do not like surprises. I expect people to tell me when things are happening, and then I hope I respond in kind and with the same regard.

"You can build up an organization, a sense of teamwork, loyalty, and hard work, but then have some fun. You can build a culture around even a portion of an organization."

What specific actions do you take, what things do you say, that build a culture of trust, loyalty, teamwork, and fun?

"One is you clearly need to make sure that you've taken care of and promoted the people who have responded to the type of culture you want. The second aspect--and this is probably one of the hardest management jobs ever, and one of the reasons I was nervous about getting into management--is that you have to fire people when they don't match that culture.

"You can build it by your actions. While I'm not looking forward to any terminations, a careful one or two where it's really appropriate and very obvious to the organization may be necessary. You lose ground--it's not like you just stay status quo--you actually go backwards when you fail to terminate, when it's clear to the organization that that person is not following what you're all saying you're about. Sometimes you have to take the hard actions in order to mold the organization and then the people coming in will have a better sense of what's expected.

"For example, when we decided at Exodus that we needed to move someone out, several of the executives came back and said they felt better about the company because we did that. Not because it was easy, but we now feel better about our company going forward, knowing that we all have the capability to execute. Sometimes you can take a very bad situation and it almost becomes a positive. Not quite, it still hurts, but it becomes a positive.

"It is very difficult when you make a decision and you do not have buy-in, so I try not to do that. Life is too lonely without that. You can make some of the tough decisions if in fact you get some buy-in from your team."

I've heard General Schwarzkopf say that one of the keys to leadership is doing the right thing. You seem to have the same philosophy.

"Integrity is extremely important. I do not know how to lie. Not answering questions, I'm getting better at. If you say I'm doing the right thing, to the extent of my knowledge or my understanding, for the shareholders, for the employees, and for the market, as in the case of shooting an operating system, you can get through that by saying it was the right thing to do. Then you can deal with yourself much better. Because many of these decisions are heart-rending decisions that do take a toll on you and your whole spirit. But if you don't make them, success is very hard to accomplish unless you've given yourself little goals. You really want to achieve something. You can't avoid these difficult decisions. They pop up whether you like them or not."

When you have a day when you question yourself, what do you do to bring yourself back into alignment?

"So much of this is really exciting and it matches what I like doing. Because this company is aligned, for example, with the types of technologies I like, I know that once I'm in the office, I'm going to get excited. I knew when I was looking for that next job, that if I found it in the right space, that it would just be a tremendous benefit for me personally. This job has allowed me to accomplish things that I said I really wanted and needed to do. I hate to think what it would have been like if I had decided after Apple that it was over. If I had ever decided to not do it and then realized I'd given up this opportunity, I probably would not be very happy."

What other types of behaviors do you have that have been integral to your success?

"Jobs like this require a tremendous energy level. It does require some understanding of delegation. It does require you to constantly have a system, a network of friends and people who are going to give you advice when you're wandering astray and not paying attention. I have friends who will say, 'Ellen, you're not paying attention to that! Just go nail that one.' And that helps. You have to listen and sometimes there are better days for listening than others. Other people have to be sensitive, too, as to whether you're ready for all the input. But listening helps. This is not for people who have a low energy level. This requires you to be up almost all the time. It did require me to have more understanding of finance. I'm pleased that in the jobs I've had in the past, while I never was in the finance department, I was required to represent the finances of my group. Because I now find myself in analyst meetings and presenting to investment advisors, representing the financial situation and services of Exodus. A lot of things prepared me for this role and yet there are some things about this role that nothing could have prepared me for.

"If you walk into these kinds of positions with a fair amount of experience base, then having instincts and counting on your instincts is first. Not needing that massive report or the task force report, but to be able to make a decision, a decisive decision based on instincts, is extremely important. And then show the leadership to your team."

I've noticed, for myself, that age has enhanced my ability to listen to my intuition. Have you found that to be true, or was there some point in your life when you said, 'That's it; I'm going to follow my instincts'?

"There was a defining moment. I can't remember exactly when it was, but I know it occurred when I finally said, 'Wait a second, why am I waiting for all this input from all these people; I know the answer. I don't need that task force report. I know what the answer is here.' It definitely added to my value content in the equation. My instincts tell me, 'Let's go this way.' You become more of a leader when you do that, rather than just rubber-stamping someone else's report."

more of a leader when you do that, rather than just rubber-stamping someone else's report."

What role have mentors played in your career?

"I believe my first mentor was the vice president who convinced me I should be going down to Charlotte. If he's coming out to California, he and his wife will call up and say, 'Ellen, do you want to go out to dinner?' I had two other mentors, both of whom I worked for at IBM. One I see almost once a month at a board meeting. He still pulls me aside and asks how I'm doing, how's the company working, what I'm working on. And that's valuable. It becomes more of a personal experience, rather than just an assignment. I try to do the same thing for other people. I have both formally and informally mentored people, because I remember some of the people who helped me when I was doing things for the first time as a female in the company. I try to leave some time in this balanced life of mine to say either 'Let's do it over e-mail' or 'Let's get together, let's chat, let's have a cup of coffee.'"

In corporate America there are a lot of "unwritten rules." What rule have you found to be the most critical one?

"There are rules in every company, whether it's small or large, and your influence on those rules changes. If you are a brand new employee in a large company, they have rules, and you really do need to know what they are and you need to know whether you're comfortable fitting into those.

"I do think it's important to understand the underlying rules, the underlying principles, and find out if you like those. Some people find them too confining.

approved? Is that what they like to see?' I usually try to be sitting in an environment before I have to go and be in front of it."

Are there days you just wanted to give up?

"Oh, quite a few. I've had them most when I'm in transition. When I left Apple and was not sure what I wanted to do next, I really did have to ask myself, 'Why am I doing this one more time? What am I trying to do?' By the way, when I'm successful, will I know it and will I know to stop?   Will I know that I've accomplished something? Sometimes we have accomplished what we thought and we don't pay attention to it."

"Understanding people--what's on their minds, what it takes to engage them in an idea and position them to be willing to work with you--is a critical skill."

JEAN HAMILTON

- **Chief Executive Officer – Prudential Institutional & Executive Vice President – Prudential Insurance Company of America**
- **Degree: Bachelor of Science – Communication Master of Business Administration**

Jean Hamilton is responsible for Prudential's group insurance, retirement services, real estate and relocation, guaranteed products and workplace marketing business units.

One of Jean's keys to success is her ability to watch others around her, to learn from what they are doing and then incorporate that into her own life. This has enabled her to continue to raise her own personal bar of performance.

How would you define success?

"Success has a lot of different parameters. Success means creation and articulation of a vision that is very strong, is customer-focused, inspirational and passionate, and that can pull together all of the members of our team toward a common set of goals. From that vision, we develop a strategy and execute against it. It's very important to link the goals of each person in the group to this overall vision. Only then can you truly achieve success.

"Personally, I love businesses. I enjoy seeing them grow and prosper. For example, I might stumble upon a great entrepreneur who's starting a fruit market and I will be unable to resist helping him or her, assuming this person wants help. I'm just drawn to seeing business ideas come to fruition. I'm lucky to have the opportunity to combine what I do in my professional life with what I feel passionately about in my personal life. Over time, I've seen both sides of my life come together around this idea of helping businesses to grow and prosper.

"I feel fortunate, because as time has gone by, my personal friends and my professional friends have merged. This has allowed me to have more balance in my life, especially since we are all starved for personal time. This blending of my professional and private relationships has made a real difference.

"When I think of success, I think of a company that has done well, a problem that was solved, a terrific person who was hired onto the team, a colleague with whom I've been working who continues to excel, and accomplishing personal goals with friends and family. Those are all things I find very valuable and rewarding."

What would you say is your success formula for having reached the top?

"I've been lucky to work with a number of people from whom I've been able to learn. I've used them as role models, carefully watching to see things they do well and to think about how I can emulate them in what I do. I set goals for myself constantly. When I see someone doing something well, I often adjust and adapt my own goals. For me and the people I work with, that constant adjusting of goals and raising the bar is something that is very important for success.

"Being open to new ideas is another important lesson. Listening to what others have to say, observing success, and then finding a way to personally incorporate that into your own set of goals and standards--all of that is critical. I've had some wonderful mentors, not only senior colleagues, but also people with whom I work or who work for me. The key is remembering to listen, understand, and incorporate all the good ideas, regardless of the source of information.

"Another important element of any formula for success is to keep your responsibilities in perspective. When you first start out in the workplace, you obviously have a lot of responsibility for specific details and specific kinds of execution. As you move up the leadership ladder, your responsibilities change and become broader.

"One of the most important things that I can do now as a CEO is to take the time to set a clear vision, strategy and goals and then find the right people to do the job. I'm a big believer in putting a great deal of effort into matching people and jobs. You also have to form strong teams so that everyone is supporting everyone else. When you do these things well, you have a formula for success."

You belong to quite a few groups and boards. What decisions do you make that allow you to bring balance to your life and still have time for these other activities?

"Balancing one's work and personal life is a daunting challenge. As a leader, you need to think carefully about how you should and can add value, which often requires delegating more. For many people, that's not easy to do. However, it is very important because it helps you stay at the right level in the work process and, importantly, it helps you achieve more balance in your life. None of us can do it all. It's also important to learn to make decisions quickly and in a timely way. This means knowing how much information you really need to make a decision without overanalyzing it. You also need to understand the market and competitive forces at work. It comes down to doing your homework, understanding the risks, making the decision--and then sticking with it. Don't be afraid to learn from your lessons. If you didn't quite do it right at first, understand why that was, and strive to do it better the next time.

"One of the most important, and often elusive, elements of balancing your personal and professional life is to give yourself some time to think and reflect. We all do that in different ways. One of the things that I have learned is to focus on the topic at hand without letting other concerns distract me. I use this technique to relax as well. I find I can clear my mind from all the problems and recharge. I also use this technique to step back from the details and say, all right, is everything still going in the right direction? Should we change our strategy? Should we do something differently? Make sure you take the time to just think.

"One way to give yourself time to think about important issues is to physically get away. There are a several places I've gone to that I find very valuable. The Center for Creative Leadership does a good assessment in a setting of a small group of peers. Another place that I very much enjoy is the Aspen Institute, which offers time to explore and integrate both your mental and physical well being. It is the combination of the two that is so valuable.

"In my personal life, physical activity is very important for my overall well being. It helps clear your mind and makes you feel good about yourself. For example, that's why I love skiing. I enjoy the exercise and the beautiful environment.

"I also recommend a healthy dose of family time. My husband and I do a lot of things together to bring balance in our lives. He works very hard as well. So we help each other by working through problems together, as well as by simply enjoying ourselves and having fun. We like to travel and we've been to a lot of interesting places. I find that the more exotic the locale--for example, places like Ecuador--the more that you stop thinking about everything that's been on your mind. You can immerse yourself in an entirely different world and in what's going on right then and there."

How have you personally changed as you've climbed the corporate ladder?

"I don't think that the essence of who I am has changed during my career. But I have found what is effective and what isn't, and, as a result, I've refined how I approach my work. Since business is about getting results, it is important to really understand the people with whom you are working and doing business. You need to think about what's in it for them, the win-win solution, not win-lose. Understanding people--what's on their minds, what it takes to engage them in an idea and position them to be willing to work with you--is a critical skill. I think that's one of the most essential skills you can strive to learn. And this doesn't mean you'll need to change as a person. Rather, it's about understanding how to work well with other people."

What other things did you have to learn?

"You need to learn new disciplines all the time. For a number of years, I was involved in making investment decisions. In that role, you make judgments about the strategy, people and characteristics of the investment that allow you to make good decisions. But when I moved over to managing businesses myself, there were some areas that I had to understand more clearly. For example, how do you really run something well from an operations and systems perspective? How do you create and drive a strong project plan? You can judge the results if you are investing in a company, but really knowing how to do it yourself requires that you learn some new technical skills. Learning needs to be a constant part of any career.

"Fortunately, I've worked with people who were quite willing to teach me. I've learned the hard way, from trial and error, too. As your career develops, you constantly need to keep in mind that most jobs are about execution and results. Remember to analyze your own work and honestly assess the results. If it didn't turn out as you'd hoped, be willing to go back and evaluate why, and how you're going to do it better the next time."

It sounds like you are definitely one who is always raising the bar for yourself. It's like, I've met that goal; maybe I didn't set it high enough--and then you raise it from there.

"I continually review and adjust my professional and personal goals. It's a healthy thing to do and the smart thing to do, especially in today's rapidly evolving workplace. Similarly, I continue to revisit and challenge our business goals, too, and I prefer to work with people with the same philosophies. So, together, we are pushing each other to the next level."

It's not necessarily choosing people who are like you, but who have a basic philosophy or value system like you have.

"The value system is what is most important. But picking people who are different from you--and different from one another--is extraordinarily valuable, particularly today. Things are moving and changing so quickly. We are faced with opportunities and challenges – both in business and in our personal lives – related to an increasingly global economy and society. The Internet is really making that happen more easily. We need to have different perspectives and diversity of backgrounds and experiences. I'm confident that this will allow us to find much better solutions. So if you look at the team of people with whom I work, we share values, goals, and standards, but we also come from very different backgrounds and we come at things in very different ways."

Were there any events in your life that prepared you to hold such a role?

"When I first started out, career paths for women were not at all clear. Fortunately, my parents were extraordinarily supportive of me. My parents worked with me, not just as their daughter, but as their child. I had so-called girls' toys and also boys' toys. We did what were traditionally considered girl activities and boy activities. Maybe that's why I never thought about only doing things the way a girl was expected to do them. The belief that my parents had in me gave me a lot of personal confidence. I really believed that I could succeed. If I needed help or support, or if something wasn't going well, they were really there for me. I can't emphasize enough how critical I believe their support was to me. I owe a debt of gratitude to my parents.

"Regarding choosing a career, I changed my mind a lot through the years. When I was quite young, the first thing I wanted to do was be a surgeon. And then I wanted to be an architect. Unfortunately, I was discouraged from both careers by my high school guidance counselors who said, 'Of course you know, Jean, you need math in those professions and girls just aren't very good at math.' Well, my career certainly proved that premise wrong. A lot of what I've done since high school has required analytics and math. Looking back, I do see a connection between what I wanted to be as a child and what I've become. In all of these professions, there is definitely an analytical component, but there's a creative, artistic component as well. A lot of business is the analytical nuts and bolts, such as making the bottom line and performing well in the market against your competitors. But there's a creative aspect to the job, too. Seeing the opportunities, setting the vision, creating the strategy, building the team and understanding how to effectively execute involves a lot of creativity."

What were your key learning lessons?

"The key learning lessons for me are understanding what you do well and what will excite you. If you don't have personal passion about something, if you don't feel confident about your ability to achieve, I don't think your career is a good match. I don't think you'll be happy. It will simply be a day-to-day paycheck.

"If the match isn't good, when it comes time to make the tough decisions, you'll be afraid to make them. You won't do what you know has to be done because you don't feel it in your heart. You won't be willing to take the risk and say this is what has to be done for the business; this is the right thing to do. It can't be about your personal risk. It has to be about what is right for that business. That is why I believe that affinity and passion for your job are absolutely key."

What role models have you had and what role have they played in your life?

"There isn't a specific individual who is my role model. I take various individuals' characteristics, successes, and ways of doing business, which I then put together in a picture that works for me. That's also consistent with the way that I think about business problems. I'm someone who picks from a variety of sources, sees a pattern, and puts it together in a fashion that works."

Do you have a particular success story that stands out in your mind?

"If I go beyond specific events, one of the most important things to me is that I've been able to be true to myself and to my standards throughout my career. If I look back and ask if I have done the right thing, the answer is yes. I feel good about what's happened in my professional and personal lives. I think for all of us, staying true to yourself, and your standards, and your ethics, means success."

What have been some of your defining moments?

"A lot of defining moments for me also have to do with ethics and standards. I work very hard to try to make things work and to always do them in the right way. I'm very loyal and I want success for the team or the group as a whole. But sometimes I will find the standards or ethics of a company or a person are incompatible with my own.   In these instances, recognizing those differences and saying it's time to move, not finding fault, but just saying this will never work, is the right approach.   If we can't have success together, then let's just let it go and move on.   I think those situations have been very defining moments for me."

Is there any particular way that you learned to let go?

"It's a matter of experience. My tendency, often out of loyalty, is to stay with a situation or problem longer than many people would. I feel a lot of ownership, responsibility, and affinity for personal and professional situations. Sometimes, I probably work too long and too hard to make some of them work out. So it's been a matter of looking back at those situations and asking if they helped me grow or if they limited my development. If the situation is limiting, no one is served by continuing with that particular effort."

As you were going up the corporate ladder, were there moments when you met resistance? How did you deal with that?

"I remember when I was first working, I was told that women really couldn't do certain jobs. Therefore, I should be happy with a lesser assignment.   I've typically listened to this rhetoric, tried to understand why the individual or company took this position, and then I quickly charted a course to prove them wrong.

"When I was first working, for example, I was in a situation where I had been given responsibility for a major account. In fact, it was the most profitable account for the organization at that time. One of my predecessors on the account told the president of that organization that I couldn't possibly be successful and we would lose the business. My first response was to try to understand why someone would be so negative. In this case, there wasn't any logical reason for the assertion that I couldn't do the job, so I concluded that some people are just wrong. Then I worked even harder to prove the person wrong. I'm pleased to report that the account continued to grow and become more profitable under my direction. I've experienced that type of situation many times in my career, but I've been very lucky that there have always been people who believed in me and who were willing to give me the opportunity to achieve or fail. They took a risk with me, and that made all the difference."

Why do you think that was--that people were willing to take that risk with you?

"People were willing to take a risk with me because they saw that I would work very hard, that I believe very strongly in things, that I would do what was necessary to make it work. If I needed help or new skills, I would find the help, get the instruction, or take the course. What drives me is finding a way to achieve. That's what matters more than anything. I'm very competitive and goal oriented. I think they saw that in me."

We all make sacrifices in life to get what we want. What kind of sacrifices have you made to reach this level?

"There are several kinds of sacrifices that I have found to be the hardest. One is that the time I have to spend with my family and friends is not what I would want it to be. That's why I began to focus on ways to be more efficient with my personal time. In fact, I began applying some of the efficiency tools that I learned from business. I started to get very aggressive about scheduling time with friends and family. It all goes on my calendar. That's the way I have to deal with things in business, so I did the same outside of the office. Using those kinds of tools helps me minimize the sacrifices. You also have to learn to say enough is enough; I need a break and I'm going to go off to do this for myself or my family. Now, I don't take my own advice as often as I should, but I try to do so whenever possible. I've had to make sacrifices, but I've tried to find ways to keep them from being overbearing.

"Certainly, there are a lot of things I would like to do that I don't get to do because of my career. Traveling, exploring, learning new things often have to be put at a lower priority. I work in New Jersey and travel a lot, so at times I feel that my home in New York is just like another hotel room. When I really start to feel this way, I make an effort to try to change my schedule to gets things back into better balance. I also recognize that there are different stages in life, so there are things that I will do at some time in the future that I can't do now."

Do you have any regrets?

"I may have a momentary regret from time to time, especially given the number of choices that one makes in a lifetime. But I try to look at the overall picture of my life. All things said and done, would I have done anything differently? I don't think that I would have. Yes, there may have been a day or a year when I would have liked things to have been different, but to me what is important is to feel that I'm a whole person who has achieved personally and professionally.

"I also don't recommend comparing your life to someone else's. They've had to make all kinds of choices themselves in different situations. It's better to ask yourself if you feel good about what you've done and where you're going. I certainly do. I think that's the way to look at it. I'm basically a very positive and optimistic person, so I try not to dwell a lot on regrets."

What are some of the major challenges that you've had to overcome?

"An obvious challenge is being a woman. There were certainly people in my career who didn't think a woman could do certain kinds of jobs. Like many women, I've had to deal with that. But fortunately for me, there was always someone more enlightened who believed that a woman could do whatever she put her mind to. I've found that I have gained great strength by going through those kinds of challenges in my career.

"One of the nice things now is to see that what had been a challenge--being a woman in a workplace run primarily by men--can now be an advantage. The workplace itself is changing. We no longer have the strict organizational hierarchies of the past. The best management style is no longer 'command and control.' The ability to form strong groups and teams, to listen, and to delegate is becoming increasingly important in business today. I think women feel comfortable with this type of management style, which can give them a distinct advantage."

Some of the comments that I hear from women are that they don't feel they are listened to or valued in the organization and they believe that comes from being a woman. What are your suggestions?

"It is important to understand what your skills are and what the requirements of the job are. It's not just a matter of working harder, spending more hours in the office, or doing more reports. It is about finding a match so that you can really achieve. It's also important to talk about your accomplishments, not in a boastful fashion, but in a way which makes them clear. Some women have been a little less willing to promote themselves. There are a lot of decisions we all have to make every day about who should be promoted or who can do the job well. Obviously, the more that we know about an individual, the more likely we will be to consider her or him. I would advise women to make sure that, in the right way, their successes in the corporation are understood."

In articles about powerful women, some of them stated that they didn't feel powerful. What are your thoughts about the power that comes with your position?

"The power that comes with any position has to be used for the benefit of the organization. I have a very hard time with people who just use it for their personal achievement. It's a matter of understanding that in order to get things done, you need to use the position in the right way. Women especially must be comfortable with that. They cannot feel that it is inappropriate to exercise their power. Otherwise, they can't possibly be successful either for themselves or for the organization for which they have responsibility."

How do you influence people to your way of thinking?

"First, you must really believe in what you're espousing. If you don't, it will be very easy for someone to punch holes in your thinking. Next, you need to clearly communicate how your point of view is good for your organization, not just good for yourself. If you don't make this point clear, others may quickly try to paint your position as self-promoting. In any business effort, the most influential path is the one that is truly a win-win situation. It's very important to understand the perspective of the person or group with whom you will be dealing. What are their goals? What are their barriers? What are they afraid of? What's really essential that they accomplish? What is it that they think about? And how do they communicate? Only then can you truly develop a win-win scenario. If you push through your position, you may have short-term success, but the solution or the partnership won't last."

Has there ever been a time when you just said, "I just want to give up, and I don't want to do this any more?"

"There have been days and moments when I may have had such thoughts. We all have those points in our lives. But I have a very long perspective on things. It is like being a good chess player who looks out, looks at the whole board, determines the game plan, and pragmatically executes to achieve success. If you strive to see the big picture, and you really want it, then you'll keep moving along the necessary paths that will get you there. Yes, there are times, there are even days or weeks, when I just need to disengage to some extent because something is particularly difficult. But those breaks help me refocus and establish better balance in my life. Take the time to reflect, and you can usually find a way to get through a problem."

There are statements made that a lot of female executives act very masculine. How do you utilize your female and your masculine side to be most effective?

"Since many women like myself had very few female executives to view as role models in business, there was a tendency to try out different styles and approaches. Many of them were taken from the male role models in both style and in dress. Let's all be thankful that's behind us. My thought process--the way I approach things mentally, intellectually--has been characterized as being more traditionally male than female. The way in which I manage and work with people is a mixture of both sides.

"On the feminine side, one should be the way that one wants to be. Clearly there is behavior or dress or other things that are inappropriate for some environments, and you have to be careful about those things. You have to be careful about the way you present yourself. But, it's rather nice to have female and male sides and to have that show in the work place. Simply put, just be yourself. I don't think there is inherent gender conflict in the workplace, especially if you remain true to yourself, while acknowledging the environment in which you're operating."

"It's all about choices and having a positive outlook. Even if you fail, you always learn something through the process."

KAREN GARRISON

- **President, Pitney Bowes Management Services**
- **Degrees: Bachelor of Science – Accounting**
             Master of Business Administration
- **Children: 2**
- **Age: 51**

Karen Garrison is responsible for the fastest growing business unit at Pitney Bowes. She provides customers with on- and off-site business support services.

Building a winning team is a key to success. Karen shares specific ideas about building a winning team that have allowed her to be so effective. You will learn the "Garrison Theory"--a theory that shows her team she cares, and yet is focused on winning.

How do you define success?

"As a leader, I define success as the teams that you build. Success is teams of people that are empowered: they have an opportunity to know where they fit in, they take pride in what they do and when they go home at night, they can tell their families or their friends, with much pride, what they do and look forward to coming in the next day. As a leader, it's really about growing people; that almost always grows your companies. As a person, it's about being able to have balance, to have your wonderful family and to be able to balance your job along with that."

How do you make that balance happen in your life? What kind of decisions do you make?

"It's really exactly what you said; it's all about making decisions, I learned very early on. I've been in the business world for 30 years now, and particularly for young women starting off, if you do not make choices about your family, about your business life, it's very easy to be consumed by the business side because you want to move up the corporate ladder. As I said, I learned very early on that my family is very important to me. I'm very proud to be a mother, to be a wife, and a sister and all those other things. I probably, at times, got myself in trouble when I would tell my boss--this was 20+ years ago--that I was taking off from work to go to my daughter's play. Today that's much more accepted. In fact, then I was probably one of the few that was open and honest about it. Many called in sick for whatever it might have been, or worse yet, did not go. But I felt very comfortable. I wanted to do it my way, which was eyeball to eyeball. It's important that I go to my daughter's play. Probably something inside of me said that if it wasn't important to them, I needed to know that."

It's amazing that the company accepted your position.

"I'm not sure if they accepted it. Part of it is personality driven. My husband and daughters would tell me that I'm the in-your-face pushy type at times. It would have been very easy to be intimidated back then. Why do you have to go to your daughter's play? Well, because I do. It's very important and I won't get a chance to do it again. I would come back with the 'why.' I did work for bosses who were wonderful, who would just smile and look the other way. I worked for some that actually encouraged it. I worked for the typical ones that thought it was ridiculous. They had never been to their daughter's play; why did I need to do that?

"But I did go. There would be the classic situation: you would go into a meeting later and all of the guys--because I would be the only female in the group of managers--the guys would have their side remarks, but it truthfully did not bother me. Many of them, I know, would have loved to have gone to their daughters' plays, but it was not accepted really for anyone back then. But I felt comfortable; that's where I needed to be so I went and ignored a lot of the words.

"As I was able to go into the ranks of supervisor and then manager, I had to be very cautious. You couldn't go to every play; you couldn't go to every soccer game. But you needed to be there for the ones you knew were the most important ones. I encouraged the people who worked for me to do the same thing. Pretty soon, I was the only department that was encouraging, not only endorsing, but encouraging. You know why? Because the work still always got done. People appreciate that; now they want to come to work in your area.

"That's the balance of life. It started early on. I got to be known not as the female manager or leader, but as the manager who encouraged that there could be a family outside of work also."

What impact does being the only woman in a meeting have?

"I don't pay any attention to that. I did, obviously, early on, when I was the first female CFO, chief financial officer. But now as a business unit president, there are usually all guys around me, and when I visit the companies, and also the customers that we work for, many of them are usually guys, but it's so business-oriented now. It's very, very rare that the female-male thing comes up. It's much more of a diversity issue. Mainly, I have been in the business long enough, that I just ignore a lot of the stuff."

What is your success formula that has enabled you to reach officer level?

"Mine started off early on with a positive outlook. Absolutely, that we could do anything. Years ago when I said I was going to run a business, a lot of people laughed. But deep inside, I really knew I would some day. You need to surround yourself with people who have not a cocky attitude, but a positive one. Every single day challenges, obstacles, come up, problems come up, but if you have people who have the right attitude, who don't necessarily know how to solve it, but we'll put our heads together, that's been the true success. I do that in my personal life and try to teach my daughters that it's all about choices and having a positive outlook. Even if you fail, you always learn something through the process. It's the one challenge that I've had, when you run departments that have many negative people in them--people can always learn, they can be trained, they can be motivated, except for the attitude. Especially, if they don't have the attitude to at least try. The biggest thing is the positive attitude. People are always telling me, how do you wake up every day with that attitude. It's just, maybe, I was born with it. I really look forward to challenges.

"The other thing is focus. It's all about focusing and when you reach manager and then you're at director level and then officer level, we have thousands of things a day that we can do--but the difference between being really successful and not, is do you focus on those things that are going to make the biggest difference and then convince the team members to focus on the right items.

"Then it's about being demanding. I read a book recently that talked about the fact that the best leaders are rigorous, demanding leaders. It doesn't mean that you're in people's faces with hollering and screaming, it means that you're demanding at keeping people focused and delivering. Not just talking about it, but really delivering. I do that really well.

"To me, it's being fair. Fairness and trust are things that I like to use, too. We're always raising the bar. It's really about telling people that we're at this stage and we're going here, and what we need--the tools, the systems, and the training. Where most companies and most leaders fail, I personally think, is that they know where they are going, but they don't paint the picture, they don't really let people know where they fit in. And worse yet, when people aren't moving at the right pace, the leaders are not demanding enough to let them know."

How have you had to change to be successful in this environment?

"Throughout the years, I have had to temper my perfectionist attitude. Not only was I positive but I was positive that I would do it absolutely right. In the early days, most of us started off as one-on-one. We were doing something very, very well and that's how we got recognized or noticed. But as you start managing people, you have to accept that you can't personally do it all, even though you might know you could do it better. You have to trust that other people can do it better. You have to give it up. You have to really, truly delegate and for those of us who really want to do a lot and do it well, that's very hard to do normally.

"Most of the leadership failures I've seen have been where people have become leaders and managers, and not really trusted and delegated so that they themselves can take on more. I tried it that way myself, on the side, at night and in the morning, I still do it, but that just doesn't work. I've learned the hard way, by either missing a deadline, which was devastating, or by not having it to the right level. Then as the years went on I started realizing I didn't need to go the fourth decimal point. The higher up you go, you understand it's all about the strategy and the vision and being close to the mark. You learn to do something really, really well versus making it perfect. I've learned to give that up also.

"Most of the people who work for me know that if you can't get it down to one piece of paper, focus and be concise and make it very clean and crisp, then move on. Sometimes you have to drill down through the 40 layers, but it's very, very rare. I had to learn not to be a perfectionist, but still to want it done right. There is a big difference there. It's important to delegate, trust and to focus."

What allowed you to back off the perfectionism and to trust that people were going to do what they said they would do?

"It's all in the caliber of people you surround yourself with. Some companies and leaders compromise and keep people around them with either a bad attitude or the wrong attitude, who do not have the right skill set, who haven't kept their saw honed, and/or do not have the right team effort. Because many times it isn't one-on-one, it is working with a team. I learned that as I surrounded myself with the very best and brightest. I usually found that when I would interview them and ask 'What do you want to do later?' the ones who said 'I want your job' were the absolute right ones.

"I would pretty soon have unbelievable teams, that I either was able to hire in or the ones that were given to us through recognition, motivation. And again, letting them know where they fit into the team can raise the bar significantly. Jack Welch is someone who I followed personally for a long time because of his success, and he breaks leaders down into four different types: the As, Bs, Cs and Ds.

"Many of us can make As, and we can be the A student. Some are just naturally bright; most of us have to study, and we have to work hard. You have to be prepared to come into class wanting to make the A. It's that attitude thing again. The Bs are the ones who can be the A, if they really put the extra effort in. The Cs I usually don't spend a lot of time on, because they've chosen that they don't want to be the B or don't want to be the A, and they're just hanging out in that comfort zone. The Ds and the others, we don't spend any time with, other than to be fair--to say, you're here, you need to be at the next point--and we try to understand what is going on in their lives and either see positive movement or move them out.

"But whether it's the Maslow theory, the Jack Welch theory, or Garrison theory that comes through, it's really about communicating with people. On my direct team, with as many people as I can touch, I feel comfortable that I know where people are in their stage of life. Sometimes you can be an A and be wonderful--you're doing your homework, you're ready for the win of the game but something happens personally, and you backtrack a little bit. That's okay. I mean all of us have times when we're an

A+ and then we're a B+ and then we're a B and then we're an A again. That's all right.

"But it also helps you understand as a leader what you need to do to help that person. You have to engage--not to be personal friends, not to be buddy buddies--but to know where people are on that gauge. Women do that better. Jack Welch obviously does it wonderfully, but women have that talent. It's part of that mothering thing that we do sometimes when we try to know where the kids are, what's going on in school, what's going on in the soccer game, and what's going on at work. But I'm finding more and more men who are comfortable with being responsible for the attitude and skill set that people are bringing to work. You really have to raise the bar. I keep using that term because once you get there, it's not okay to hang out; it keeps being raised and raised, whether it's by local or global competition."

When you have the Ds, do you fire them?

"I usually move them out of the organization. Absolutely, if you want to be a winning team. I only want to be on winning teams. I am not ashamed to say that. You come in totally, differently prepared than if you just want to be doing it for the fun. The D players are not coming to be on the winning team. Sometimes, unfortunately, it's because of their own skill set, because of the level that they've gone to school, their lack of credentials, or whatever it might be. They are in the wrong job. It is not the right fit. It is not always their issue, and to keep them in there is absolutely not okay. My background has been that most managers and leaders try to walk around that."

Let's just shuffle this person.

"Exactly. Move them to someone else. Not ever look them in the eye and tell them they're a D player; instead give them an average rating because you don't want to go through all the paperwork for that.

"Or worse yet, you don't want to have to face it. It will pull the whole team down. It will not be fair to either. If you really want to be in a win-win situation, you have the hard discussion. Sometimes it's very hard, because the person has a great personality--they bake the cakes for birthdays--but they're truly not contributing to winning. You have to look at them and be very honest with them. I've had some cases where they've gone to school at night and they've been able to raise the bar. They've asked the team for different assignments, not to find a comfort zone, but to find a win-win. But most of the time, when they're a D player, it's truly that it's not the right fit and the person needs to go do something else."

You said early in your career that you wanted to be the president of the company. What events in your life prepared you for that sort of position?

"I'm not sure if I was prepared for it then, when I had said I was going to do that."

When was it that you said that?

"About 15 years ago. Pitney Bowes has a process: they look down throughout the organization to see where the bench strength is. We look three and four and sometimes five layers down; at that point, I was probably five or six layers down. I was the controller at Dictaphone Corporation which was owned by Pitney Bowes. I had been recognized as one of the future leaders, which means that you fill out your forms and do your resume. One of the forms asked, 'What would you like to do in two years, five years, 10 years and 15 years.' I filled out that from Controller, I'd like to be worldwide controller, and then I'd like to be the CFO of

Dictaphone, which itself would have been a huge move. Then I said the next move was to run a business unit. I didn't laugh at all when I filled it out. Did I really think it was going to happen? Oh, probably not. But at the same time, deep down inside, I probably knew if I was able to continue to learn as much as I'd learned--I worked with wonderful bosses, mentors, had finished my MBA--I really was poised for it. But 15 years out, who would have known.

"I definitely wanted it, just because I have the controlling personality that likes to run things and control things. But more importantly, it wasn't about making money. It truly was about running an organization that would enable me to touch people's lives. People are very important, and that's part of my payback theory that I've been absolutely blessed with. I wanted the opportunity to be able to run a company the way I would run it, which means really touching the people.

"After I turned the forms in I got a call to come up to corporate and they had, I think it was, a corporate psychologist who would interview you. At that time I had very long blond hair, it was down to my waist, and this was in the era when it would be the very manly cut if you were even thinking of going to corporate. Not me: I walked in, I had a ponytail actually, and the psychologist and I talked for about an hour. Afterwards, HR met with me the next day and said the intelligence tests that I had taken, the IQ tests, were fine, I could run with the big dogs. However, I was too enthusiastic. Now, I would have called that positive. But back in those days, it was still the very corporate thing. They were definitely keeping me on the slate, they would be grooming me and all, but they said that I was probably too enthusiastic as I looked forward to some of those events, so I just smiled. That was okay, because it wasn't really the right time. But I knew the time would be right later. I was offered the job as worldwide controller a couple of years after that.

"Actually the president of Dictaphone at the time had talked to me and told me not to take the worldwide controller's job. He said, 'Let me give you a little piece of advice. Taking one of these jobs and moving up to corporate, leaving Florida, moving up to Stamford, Connecticut, will be a huge move for your family, so don't accept the job for this job. Think at least two jobs out, whether this job positions you for whatever you eventually want to do.' Then he said, 'What do you eventually want to do?' And I said, 'I'd like your job.' He chuckled and said that I would probably get it some day. And he said, 'If that's what your goal is, then yes, you should be CFO first and before you're CFO, you should be worldwide controller. So it does fit in, if that's what your plan is.'

"The family made a huge move. My oldest daughter was starting at the University of Florida. That would have been the right time. My youngest daughter was only going into second grade. That again was the right time as far as moving children. But my husband was leaving a job where he had worked for 20 years. I was concerned more about him volunteering to quit, agreeing to move to Connecticut. I asked if that was what he really wanted to do and he said it was such an opportunity. He said, 'You're the one that really gets this stuff and really, really loves it. You have the opportunity to go for the brass ring.' He said, 'I love what I do, but I'm not on the same track that you are. I don't have the passion that you have for that.' He supported me completely and we made the move.

"The reason I'm sitting here is because I'm the president of one of the companies. I am the president of a Fortune 500 company only because I had the family behind me--truthfully. I had a wonderful company I worked for, wonderful support, wonderful programs for women, but I still would have not had made it through, as tough as that it is for me to say, unless I had the family behind me. Because there was travel, there were choices that I had to make, and mine were much easier to make because I had a complete support system."

What were the sacrifices that you had to make?

"When I was going to night school to get my MBA. Only males had graduated from the executive master's program at that point. I knew the dean of the school of business--he came to see me, Dr. Manley. He is absolutely wonderful, he was one of my wonderful mentors, but he said, 'Karen, I would love for you to be in this program, you need to crack whatever is going on.'

"We went on Saturdays and Sundays, and I had to get up early in the morning to do my homework. I got up at 4:00 and 4:30 in the morning, so I wouldn't impact my family in the evenings because I was still working full-time. Now doing this executive master's program was a little bit of an extra burden, knowing you're the only female going through it. And none had graduated. Two had actually started the program, but both had dropped out. I didn't think about it a lot, but it was still there--I wanted to make sure that I broke through and allowed other women to come. Now, I'm a naturally early riser to begin with, but I must admit there were many mornings I would have much preferred to have slept in instead of getting up and going to the dining room table. That was a personal sacrifice. I would have loved to have been playing golf with my husband on a Saturday morning, staying home and playing with my children, rather than heading off to school. But I knew it was very important for me personally to get the master's degree if I really wanted to be president of that company some day, that it would be silly of me to do that without getting the right educational background. So, I did."

What do your daughters have to say about your sacrifices?

"My oldest daughter--who lives in Florida and has three little children now--has shared with me now that she's a young woman and has matured into a wonderful mother, that she looks back and she was so very, very proud of the choices that I made. How she knew that when I needed to be there, I would be. With my youngest daughter, who is in junior high school, it's the exact same thing. They realize that Mom was getting up early in the morning to do the homework and it was transparent to them, then, but now that they are older, they sit back and say when did you do all that homework? How did you do all of that? Oh my goodness. Now I realize."

What have been the major learning lessons in your career?

"Again, it really revolves around people. The biggest lesson that I've learned is the power of what people can really do when they're open and honest and trustful. Sometimes people look at that as being soft. It's very, very strong. The teams that truly deliver results, that truly execute, come from the power of that capital asset. I learned as I went up through the financial ranks-- and I was, very good at finance and I surrounded myself with the absolute best--that the strength of the company was not balance sheet numbers, it was the people of that company and who you hang out with. That is the biggest lesson I learned. Do not compromise on the caliber and quality of the people.

"The second thing I learned is about the focus. Focus on the customers. Early on, again, about 20 years ago, I felt very comfortable looking outside and saying wait a minute, we're all here because of the customer. Unless you're working for a non-profit organization, we're here to make money. The people who write our checks are our customers. I was blessed, but I learned very quickly to work on that, to really hone that, because to have the inside outlook is just terrible. Because then you learn to do things better and quicker and cheaper, but you're still focusing inside. When you look outside and then focus outside in, and then you get your teams to think like that, it is a different person who usually comes to that team who really feels comfortable delivering something versus just hanging out. That's the type of team that I run. Try for results, feel very good about that, be competitive. So that's what I learned. Do not shy away because you're a woman from competing and being aggressive and as for some of the comments on the side, ignore them and just keep right on moving. I just pretended like I didn't hear it and just kept right on going.

"There was only one time I did not ignore comments, because it was 25 years of me ignoring a lot of stuff, and it was one of my peers. It's when I was controller and there was a peer that was very, very bright, had a lot of power and just didn't like women. He basically said that women should be home having babies and was very vocal about that. I tried to ignore it but it was really degrading. I reached the point that one day I walked into his office and shut the door and looked him straight in the eye and said, 'Number one, what you're doing is not legal; the company could have a huge lawsuit because of you. I would personally never sue you, but you are opening the company up to great liability here. You're very smart, so why are you doing it? What's your problem? It's not my problem; it's yours.' He said he didn't think women should be in the work force. I said, 'We are. Accept it. Let me tell you something: if you keep talking like this then I will go to the next level, because it's not acceptable and I'm not going to take it for myself or for the others. So clean up your act. What you want to do at home is great, but what you do here is not acceptable. It's not professional.' It's the only time I've ever really used a threat. Afterwards, he said that I needed to leave his office, and I did.

"But at the next meeting, he didn't vocally make any smart aleck comments; he just sat there and believe it or not, over the next year, we actually got to be almost friends. We never got to be real friends but at least he had accepted that I had the guts to walk in there. He did clean up his act. Later I had some women come and thank me for that. I mainly did it because I was mad.

"Later I realized we have to be prepared to step up in uncomfortable situations like that, which are confrontational actually. After I did that, I felt much, much more comfortable and he quite frankly was a much better team member. I don't think anyone had ever stepped up to him before. But he was smart enough to realize that he was out of line. That one worked well."

Have you experienced breaking through a glass ceiling?

"We are cracking through. I used to always say you don't want to crack the glass ceiling, you want to melt it. But sometimes you have to take the sledgehammer and you do have to whack it a couple of times."

When did you do that?

"I do consider one of those times to be when I had the one-on-one meeting with the gentleman. I really consider that a whack, not so much at the glass ceiling, but at the male/female thing. The glass ceiling, I haven't whacked at it. I have at the walls, as you go up to the glass ceiling. It's usually harder to get through the glass walls, I personally think, than it is to get through the glass ceilings. When you work with people who are your peers--whether it is in engineering, marketing, sales, finance--most of those power leaders are going to be males still today. You can get on teams with them, committees with them. You can deliver for them. If they are the right leaders, whether you're male or female is not going to matter, it's going to be that you deliver results, the right way. That then will allow you, as you start breaking those barriers down, to go to the next and the next. If you think you're going to go straight up through the middle, I have found that really doesn't work. You need to have the teams around you.

"Women sometimes work very smart, graduate from the best schools, but come out with that almost toughness, that idea that they are just going to punch right through. One of my bosses told me I had the ability to hit someone in the stomach with a velvet glove and that person would smile. I do not holler and scream. I don't kick down walls or anything, but at the same time, I'm very effective with staying right on focus, delivering what needs to be delivered, calling people on it when they're off the mark, when they're not delivering. If you can do that, then you will start moving, because that's what companies are screaming for right now."

What is your greatest success?

"My greatest success is being a mother of two wonderful daughters and one granddaughter and two grandsons. Having daughters that are very self-reliant, young women that like themselves. That's the greatest pride that I take. My husband and I worked very hard to love them, but also to give them space.

"I'm the president of Pitney Bowes Management Services, and I'm very, very proud of that, but it's something that I do, it's not what I am. That's where women have to be very careful, too--they can get wrapped into the job and that becomes what they are rather than what they do. I've seen some very sad stories come out of that.

"I'm most proud of being a great mom--I work hard at it--and second being a great president, because I work hard at that, too."

A study about male executives[11] states that they view their identity in terms of the role of president of the company rather than as a personal identity.

"I reached a point a couple of years ago and I said, you know what, I might not be president, because at that point, it's really timing, you have to have the right spot open up. Even though you're on the slate and I knew that I was on the slate, it wasn't guaranteed at that company that I would be president. I had become very, not satisfied with, but accepting of the fact that I didn't have to be president, even though I still wanted the opportunity to run my own company. I knew that I could do it, I knew that I should do it, but if the timing didn't happen, that was okay. When you can reach that point, it's very fulfilling. I do feel sorry for people who are still push, push, push because they focus so much on pushing. They are either not having fun--which is really important, you need to keep doing that--or they are not allowing themselves to do the best for their company, because they are so wound up in their personal things. It's so important that you keep who you are and what you do separate."

What are some of the defining moments in your life?

"I married very, very young and my husband and I had been dating as teenagers, we got married as teenagers, and in the mid-60's we wanted to go to Florida. My mom and my sisters and brother lived in Florida; we were up in Virginia. We could have stayed in Virginia where you went to work for the local factory or local whatever, but we were ready to break away, wanted to come down and help my mom. My dad had died, and she had all these children and we wanted to come and help her. But we also wanted to be part of putting a man on the moon. We packed our car with $50 to our name, and drove to Satellite Beach, Florida. You would immediately have 10 or 15 job offers that actual day.

"It was a bustling area; everything was growing, brand new. We left an area that was steeped in tradition where you were almost

programmed: you were born here and you will do this. We went to Brevard County where people were coming in from all over the world: it was a melting pot, it was diversity, it was all ages and it was we're going to put a man on the moon. There was a mission.
I didn't really think about it until about 10 years later, but everyone in the community, whether you were janitor, a secretary, an engineer, knew what their mission was, where they fit in.

"The companies that we worked for were very positive thinkers. There was a lot of youth; there were a lot of young people. It wasn't about age, it was about attitude. When someone asks me, 10 or 15 years later, why I think we can do anything, I say, we were a part of putting a man on the moon. That was a very defining time period, maybe not moment, but time period, when you were absorbed into a community that just knew. They didn't know how, but they knew they could do it, figure it out. That was exciting, to be part of that.

"The other defining moment was when my youngest daughter was in second or third grade. My husband and I were both traveling and we realized it was not going to work. We didn't want her in childcare. We were traveling too much. She was getting to the age of having ballet lessons, the Brownies and all of that. He and I talked and decided that even though we moved here for me to take a corporate job, I was ready to drop out for a couple of years until Ashley was older. After we talked, he said, 'No, I am volunteering,' and he said he had missed so much with our oldest daughter, and this would give him a new opportunity. He said that also I was the one who had the chance for the brass ring. That was a really defining moment for me to let him do that. I started feeling a little bit guilty, wondering if this was something I should do, or if he should quit his job. He did quit, but he does his investments, he plays golf, and he drove the kids to their games and he went on their field trips. He absolutely loved it. My oldest daughter asked him why he didn't do that when she was little.

"It was just as important that I let him do it. Even though he was doing it for me and for the family. I wasn't the least bit worried about if it would work out, because I knew that as a couple, since we were teenagers, we had made things work out. But it has been wonderful that he's Mr. Mom and I'm Mrs. President."

You mentioned several mentors. What role have they played in your life?

"It's been huge and they've all been men, because as I was coming up, there were not any women coming up. When I was graduating from high school, you would be secretary or you'd be a teacher or you'd be a nurse and the wild ones would be flight attendants, right? Stereotyped. I have had wonderful guys along the way who recognized something inside of me because I was bold enough to talk about what I wanted to be--a supervisor or a manager; I wanted to run a company.

"Earlier I mentioned Dr. Manley--I never worked for him but I was associated with him as he was the dean at the business school at F.I.T., a wonderful influence. I remember one particular time. I was having a very stressful time at work, and my daughters were at a stressful age, and it was almost too much to manage. I remember sharing with Dr. Manley that I had the chairman of the company flying in for a meeting down in Florida. I had the quarterly close going on, my daughter had a ballet recital, and I had some big schoolwork coming up. Everything was converging at the same point. When I was talking to Dr. Manley about it, he said, 'Karen, the decision is really simple.' And I said, 'You think it's simple; it's pretty complicated.' He said that if you were sick and in the hospital, around your bed would be your family--and Dictaphone Corporation, as a building, wouldn't be there, so probably the chairman wouldn't be there. Nothing against the chairman, but in your life, the most important thing is your family. I said that of course it was. He said, 'Why are you struggling with this?' I actually went to the corporate meeting, but I didn't do the homework; I just dropped that completely. At the meeting I told the chairman that I needed to leave early and that I was going to my daughter's recital, and he had a daughter who was in ballet and he started asking me all kinds of questions about the classes and everything. Again, it was one of those times when I was struggling with something that really wasn't that hard at all.

"I think back to the comment he made a lot and it is unfortunate: how when people have an illness or they lose someone, they say how it changed their whole life. Why do we have to have an event like that to change our whole life? When I'm mentoring younger people, I tell them to act like that event happened right now and think and feel it through and make those decisions right now instead of sacrificing family and all those things.

"The guy I work for right now, Mr. Marc Breslawsky, who's the COO with Pitney Bowes, has over the last 15 years been a wonderful influence on me. He taught me to focus on really key, critical items, and it was a tough way. He was very, not screaming-and-hollering tough, but almost to the point that if you brought something in and it wasn't right, you could tell by his look that it wasn't right. Before I go into a meeting now, I think of the questions that will be asked, because they will be very good questions. Otherwise, it's 'Why didn't we think of that!?'

"A really quick story--when my oldest daughter was in college, she had some surgery that turned out to be very, very serious. I had flown from Connecticut down to Florida and I was CFO at Dictaphone at that time. My boss, Marc, who was the president, was in Japan on some business and it just happened to be the end-of-the-month closing. I was calling back to the office and they were closing the books. I was at Pamela's bed and I had five doctors around consulting about whether they were going to do surgery or not and Marc called. He said, 'Tell me how things are going.' I went into the corporate mode and I started rambling numbers off to him from the closing, it was a very important close. As I started giving him the numbers, I could hear him, even though he was thousands of miles away, kind of a sigh, and he said, 'Karen, I don't care about the numbers, I'm calling to find out about Pam.'

"Again, it was just one of those moments that heightened my own sense that people do value relationships, families, and it is important. After I gave him an update on Pam, I said, 'Now do you want to know about the numbers?' and he said no, he knew I was taking care of them."

You've mentioned some of what I call the "unwritten rules." What other things do people need to know about?

"Don't go and get a mentor who may be one of the power people, and who is just politically correct. I wanted to mentor with the one who was really passionate about taking care of the customers, passionate about standing up.

"I have people walk up to me and say, 'I know you're very busy, but can I have a little bit of time.' We will work out whether it's through e-mail, voice mail, live on the phone, having lunch together. What I found is that when people are forward enough, or serious and passionate enough, to do that, then I'm going to choke a little bit of time out to help them.

"Normally then, when we get to that point, I ask them what their goals are in life. I'll say, have you written it down? Have you thought about what you really want to do? Is the next job the right job to lead you where you want to be, or do you need to think about the next two jobs? Maybe you need to move over to marketing, or out of finance and over to an operational job, or go through the line to a staff job.

"Many companies now have committees and teams. They have a lot of value and you get to network with others. Then you've got to ask yourself if you've got your educational background, if you've done what you needed to do, if you have the right attitude and passion. Do you read a lot? I read books every single week. Some of them I just skim to see if I want to go back and read them through, but you should be able at least to skim them, to pick up the different points."

How do you influence people to your way of thinking?

"I am very in-your-face forceful. I am told, at times, that I need to listen more and listen to the opinions of others, which I treasure, but I'm usually focused on where I want to go, and people just need to go with me. I use my position to be able to have the network around me of not only my own executive team, but the next two and three layers down. I spend a lot of time going out and meeting people at different levels because of the power of listening--I have worked very hard at being a better listener--but the power of listening is then to have the power to do something about it. That's something that I take very, very seriously. What can have a big effect in influencing people is if you listen to them and then you actually do something about it."

Was there ever a time when you said, I can't do this any more?

"As I think back over the last 30 years, there are probably only a couple times that I was truly thinking about giving up and moving into a different company. As long as you can make a difference, in my book, then you just keep plugging away. There were a couple of times in the last 30 years when I felt like I was in a corner and I couldn't make a difference. I was ready to give it up. I hung on a little bit longer and guess what, sometimes the players change or else I changed the players by moving to a different level. But that's the only thing that has really made me feel super stressed-- when I couldn't contribute. When you're just told to just do what you do, versus being creative and making a difference. With the teams, I try to unlock the power so they not only know where they fit in, but they can make a difference, and then it's just the sky's the limit--go do it."

Would you do anything differently?

"When I was younger, even though I spent a lot of time with my family and it was always the first priority, I would have squeezed out even more time with them.

"I would also move faster in some areas, as I worked maybe three years and then would get a promotion, three years and three years-- I probably would have been much more aggressive, if I had known what I know now. After a year and a half in some of the jobs I was in, I had already mastered it and I could and should have moved on. Not just for me personally, but for the company also. People look at my career and think I really moved fast, but I moved slowly in some areas. I would have changed that.

"I would have cut some more personal time out to have played more golf, to have traveled a little bit more. But when you're in the midst of moving up the corporate ladder, having those big deadlines, that's not even on your radar screen. But you reach a point when you realize that you can juggle that just a little bit more."

"Each event in our lives and each experience that we have helps us get to the next one. The important thing is to learn from them and go from there."

LIZ FETTER

- President and Chief Executive Officer, NorthPoint Communications
- Degrees: Bachelor of Arts – Communications
          Master of Science – Industrial Admin.
          & Public Policy
- Children: None
- Age: 41

L iz Fetter was one of the youngest officers appointed at Pacific Bell and then moved to a corporate officer position at US West.

Liz made a career change from a consulting firm to a very large, corporation. She provides insights into why and how she made that successful transition. One of the keys to Liz's success is her attitude and how she sustains an attitude for success. She has a strong belief in herself that if something is possible, she can do it. Liz has positive questions, taped to her mirror, that she asks herself each morning to get her day off to a great start.

When you started your career with Pacific Bell, how did you come into the business and then become a corporate officer?

"I had almost ten years of business experience out of business school before coming to Pacific Bell. I joined the company in 1991, after being recruited in by the Chief Financial Officer to head up Strategic Planning, which is roughly what I had been doing as a management consultant just prior to that. So I came in on a lateral move--doing what I had done as a consultant with many large companies. I came into a staff position--but a very good one--to get an overview of the business, Strategic Planning.

"Shortly after I joined the company, about eight months or so, I was told I needed to get a 'real' job. My first question was, what do you mean a real job? I was told it was something in Operations, where I'd learn how the company made money, a line function. So I was put in charge of Business Sales for a while and then went from there. I was very excited, a few years later, to have the opportunity to run a multi-billion dollar line of business as an officer. After getting some brief experience in a number of different functions, I was promoted early in my Pacific Bell tenure."

What was your success formula that allowed you to make officer level?

"It's different for each person. For me, I believe that it was doing exceptionally well at whatever was put in front of me. I had a number of very different kinds of jobs--staff positions, finance, sales, marketing. In each one of those, I tried to be exceptional. For example, in the sales position, I turned the worst-performing unit into the best performing unit in the space of ten months.

"I love challenges. Give me a turn-around and I'm really happy."

"I believe at Pacific Bell, having the senior executives feel that you're a part of the team, that you're committed to the business, is equally important as your performance results. That's true at many large companies at the senior levels. I made a critical decision in 1993, when Pacific Telesis was spinning off its wireless business (AirTouch) and I was recruited to go there and decided not to.

"I actually asked the CEO at Pacific Telesis what I should do and he said absolutely stay with the company. Don't go to AirTouch, because we're losing a lot of talent, etc., and so I came back and told him why I had chosen to stay. Shortly thereafter, he supported my being promoted to an officer position. I believe that demonstrating my loyalty, but not keeping it a secret, was really important."

What caused you to decide to leave the business a few years later?

"The primary cause of my departure was that there were fewer opportunities for me personally. In early 1997, SBC (Southwestern Bell), another big telecom player, bought Pacific Telesis. It was described as a merger, but in fact, was an acquisition. Early on, the officer team of Pacific Telesis was assured that they would get opportunities, that there was a place for everyone in the business.

"Unfortunately, my opportunities were very different in nature from what I had been doing. I had been running a multi-billion dollar line of business, reporting to the President and CEO of Pacific Bell for three years. The two positions that I was offered were essentially staff positions or running cost centers. I was also required to move from California to Texas. Previously in my career I'd made a decision that Texas wasn't one of the places where I would want to live. A combination of a lack of opportunities that were in line with my experience base, what I wanted to do, and the required change of location led to my departure."

What made you decide to go to US West?

"I did something for me that was very unusual. I actually violated one of the cardinal rules. I quit my job before I had another job.

"While I was still at SBC, one day I decided that I was going to leave. And so I did. I commenced interviewing with a number of smaller companies in the San Francisco bay area, but had been recruited by the top management of US West for some time, probably a six-month time period. Once I became available, they were very aggressive and asked me to come in to run the Consumer Services business and to live in Denver. I decided that sounded like a wonderful opportunity for both a change of venue and also for getting into the consumer side of the business, since I had been in business-to-business organizations prior to that."

It didn't seem like you were there very long. What happened?

"While there, I assessed that US West would probably not remain independent for more than about two years, from the beginning of 1998, given the industry dynamics. And thus, like many of the officers there, I had a change of control contract--a clause in my contract which means if they're bought by someone else, you get cashed out of options and money, etc. I felt that was very important, to be fully protected, having gone through one acquisition already.

"I thought I'd have a two to three-year stint there, at least in that position. Consumer Services was large, 10,000 people and five billion in revenue. It was US West's largest business unit and it was certainly meaty enough to keep me occupied for a couple of years. But about 13 months after I was in Denver, happily working away at my job, enjoying US West and that part of the country, I got a call from an executive search firm asking if I'd like to become the President and Chief Operating Officer of a pre-IPO company focused on broadband services. It was an opportunity too good to pass up."

How would you define success?

"The definition of success certainly has changed for me over the course of my life since I first got out of school. I would currently define it as feeling at peace with myself, very comfortable in my own skin. For me, it's having the time flexibility to be able to visit with my family, travel a bit, and do some of my avocations. Feeling as though there are only opportunities in the world and not a lot of downside. It's much more a mind-set than anything related specifically to wealth, material things or even where I live."

What caused that change to happen?

"That change was the result of a combination of some things that happened in both my personal life and business life. When SBC acquired Pacific Telesis, I realized that the opportunities in front of me were really up to me. I had built up this long tenure and track record of success at one company, it was purchased by another, and suddenly I was a second-class citizen. That was a big awakening which has served me very well in the last three or four years.

"Second, I went through a divorce after being married for about five years. That was a big disappointment.

"The third thing that happened around that time was a cousin died of breast cancer at age 32.

"Those three events reinforced that time is a very fleeting thing and I really need to do what makes me happy and feel a sense of success in each moment rather than waiting for something."

It's amazing sometimes what it takes for us to have that wake-up call.

"Yes. Each of us has opportunities for wake-up calls; many times we don't recognize them and plow right through with what we're doing.

"It was a time for me, with a few months off from work, to let a lot of things sink in, look around and do some reassessing of what would make me happy in my life going forward."

Balance is important in life. What kind of decisions or choices do you make that bring balance into your life?

"It's always a challenge. I don't know that I'm the best at it! But I really do take time for myself. Certainly, with business trips, I tag on visits with family and friends which I find allows me to feel as though I'm not just always on a treadmill. My family lives back on the East Coast and I travel a lot to New York and Boston and other cities there. By tagging on a weekend to visit them, I feel as though I don't live so far away.

"Doing things that I really enjoy is always a treat. I love to bicycle. I'm also an avid antique collector and I love remodeling. I guess melding some of my interests into the time that I have and making sure that I don't go too long without doing something that I really enjoy keeps me somewhat in balance."

We all have to make sacrifices in our lives to get what we want. What sacrifices have you had to make?

"I would say probably the biggest sacrifice that I have made is waiting to have children. I've waited quite a while. I would've had them when I was married in my mid-thirties, had that marriage not deteriorated. But that's really a deferment. I'm calling it a deferment."

What would have to happen for you to make the decision to go ahead and make a commitment and have a family and fit that into your already very busy schedule?

"I have a life plan. In fact, my mother told me a funny story a few months ago. She called me shortly after I had moved to NorthPoint and she said, 'Honey, I just discovered why it is that you have been so successful in your job.' I said, 'Why's that, Mom?' And she said, 'I went up to the attic,' (she lives in an old farmhouse in Pennsylvania, where I grew up, where the attic is a storage area for treasures) 'and I found this little notebook from when you were ten years old and it has a life to-do list in it.' Which I, of course, don't remember anything about.

"I was making to-do lists even at ten, which explains quite a bit about me! I would like to work for a few more years full-time doing what I'm doing right now and then get out of the corporate environment and do some board work, maybe do some investment and advisory work, that type of thing. But I'd like a more flexible schedule, so I'll be able to go into the next phase of my life focusing on family. Both my own family and my nieces and nephews."

It sounds almost like the first half of your life and the second half of your life.

"I have a couple of chapters; my tempo is roughly every five years for a change. In my late teens and early 20's I completed formal schooling, through graduate school. From my early to late 20's was an era of work and of life, the next stage was early to mid-30's and most recently is the phase I'm in now. I really hold the view that I'm coming into my prime."

What have been the defining moments in your life?

"I've probably had three to five moments that I really remember and at the moment knew were important.

"When I was very young, before I went to school, I realized, and this was largely a gift that my parents gave me, that I could do anything that I wanted to in the world. I had a very, very clear sense of that. I would actually tell people that too, which was probably half obnoxious, half kind of cute. Perhaps I'm hoping it was kind of cute! But my parents say, 'Oh yes, from very young you would say how you were going to do this and do that.' So when I was three or four years old, I remember that.

"When I was a young teenager, 13 or 14, I realized that I wanted to live my life on a world stage versus staying in rural Pennsylvania. It's a lovely place to visit, but I felt that I must have been adopted because I was dropped into this family that clearly was in the wrong location and I was going to be living my life somewhere very different.

"There have been a few others, but getting some real clarity about the possibilities early on in my life has made a big difference in terms of what I'm willing to take on."

How have you learned to be effective with people?

"A couple of things that I focus on make a difference. I certainly have had my own share of good bosses and bad bosses, like everyone. One of the things I believe, and offer to the people who work for me, is an opportunity to be a part of a big success-- whether that's a part of a unit within a larger company or a company like NorthPoint that is driving a whole new category related to the Internet.

"I am able to recognize what people are good at, what they like to do, and then say, 'Hey, here's a great job for you.' I also communicate and give people feedback. I also promise them that they'll be positioned for the next level shortly into their job tenure if the results are there."

Within every corporation, there are "unwritten rules." What are the rules you uncovered that allowed you to be so successful?

"I'll use Pacific Bell as an example. The situation there in 1991 was that most all of the senior and middle levels of executives had grown up there. I was coming in at a fairly senior level, just below officer, along with about six or seven other individuals who came in around the same time. Within 18 months, all of them were gone except for me. I started asking people why. I thought, am I just the dumb one here and they're all smart or what? The kind of feedback and observations that people had were: (a) Don't be too arrogant coming in. (b) Really listen to others and value the experience base. Develop teams that have experienced individuals from inside the company who have been there for a long time as well as some people from outside the company who have some fresh ideas and other experience. (c) But primarily really respect other people and hold their opinions as valuable. A very common mistake for anyone coming into a company is being a bit of a bull in a china shop and creating so much damage to relationships that it's impossible to recover."

What enabled you to come in at such a senior level into a large corporation?

"It was the familiarity that the executive who recruited me had with my work. I had been at a senior level in the consulting firm as well. In fact, I took a 35% cut in pay. At the time, I was taking a chance that I could be successful in a whole different kind of environment and that it would be worth it. And indeed it was."

How did you rise so quickly within the consulting firm?

"I think through producing results. Consulting is a very, very results-oriented business. A real meritocracy. I was very good with clients and also very good at delivering large projects successfully. In fact, I spent almost two years in Australia, setting up the Australian office for the company and building it very quickly into a multi-million dollar line of business. At the time, I felt I was a natural in consulting and frankly had some questions in my mind about whether I could be successful at other things."

Quite a change and a large risk along with the pay cut.

"It was a big risk in terms of career. Friends of mine who know my temperament could not believe I was going to the 'phone company.' Things have changed quite a bit since 1991 in telecommunications and now people wouldn't say that at all. But at that time, things were still pretty stodgy and I had gone from a very small, fast-growth consulting firm where I was running big projects and working with boards of directors and CEOs to burrowing away in some cubicle. It was a big risk, but it was a part of a plan to get the experience to be able to run a business. I wouldn't be able to do that in consulting, not be able to make that transition easily into a more senior level."

Would you consider that your biggest challenge or have you had a bigger challenge?

"Oh, boy! I've had a lot of big challenges. That was probably my biggest challenge in the last eight or nine years. The biggest challenge was making the necessary modifications in my approach from a really high-growth, very fast-moving consulting firm, working with very smart, motivated, ambitious people who were moving at light speed, into an environment that wasn't moving that quickly. Where there were a lot of people who were just putting in their time until they retired. And acting as a change agent, without burning myself out or burning too many bridges."

Do you have a specific philosophy about attitude?

"I do. I have always liked inspirational quotes. I'm not sure who said this, but one of my favorites is, *'If you know how to swim, it doesn't matter how deep the water is.'* That really captures my attitude, that with some confidence and some basic capabilities, you can take on a lot of challenges and be successful."

What type of things do you say to yourself?

"I really do feel that if it's humanly possible, I can do it. Whatever 'it' is. I will probably never be a Ph.D. in physics, a super model, or go to the Olympics, but in my chosen field I really think I can be an exceptional performer. It's a combination of early belief systems that I got from my parents and constantly pushing myself. I do have some key questions that I ask myself. I have a little list of key questions that I have taped to my mirror in the bathroom that I read every day."

Like?

"Like, what am I most proud of today? Or whom do I most enjoy being with today? They're all very positive questions and that helps me to keep on track. Particularly when the schedule is getting off track, the weather's bad, something hasn't happened that should've happened and I'm feeling a little cranky."

Were there times that you said, I've had it, I just want to give up?

"There have been plenty of times I wanted to give up. Plenty of times! But one of the most important things I have learned, I learned when I was in college. I was putting myself through school. My parents were divorced and we didn't have the money to pay for five kids to go through college, so I had to work my way through school. During two of the summers I sold dictionaries door to door in the South.

"That was a good experience in terms of teaching me the ability to every single day plug away and to be successful. I lived in the town of Decatur, Alabama, which if you remember was big during the Civil Rights Movement. Not the most progressive place in the country in terms of attitudes, particularly about girls from the North. My job was to have 30 sales calls a day. The formula was if you called on 30 people, generally housewives, you would sell three sets of dictionaries. These dictionaries were $50 a pop, so they weren't like big encyclopedias, they weren't thousands of dollars.

"Every single day, in about 100-degree heat and about 100-degree humidity, I would walk with a suitcase, carrying my books door to door. I got so many doors slammed in my face! Within two weeks everyone on my team, all 17, quit, except for me. I said, "I'm going to slug it out." And so I did. I did it for ten weeks and learned a lot about myself, and in giving up and not giving up and how it's so important to really show up, show up every day and that's probably one of the most important things that I learned. Show up and do what you're supposed to do and things will work out."

That's a great lesson to learn very early in life. How many books did you sell in a day? Did you make your three?

"I did, generally, make my three. The second summer I made almost $10,000 clear in ten weeks. That was a lot more than I had made on waitress tips the summer before, and quite a bit of money in 1979."

Since corporations are male-dominated and research has suggested that men and women do think differently, what did you do to be able to be valued, respected and listened to?

"I probably had learned some of the hardest lessons prior to coming into the telecommunications business in 1991. And that was in management consulting.

"I'll never forget being in Australia, which has a culture that's probably about 20 years behind that of the United States. I'll never forget being in a manufacturing plant with the foreman and his team where we were doing an operations study. I was asked if I could please walk up the ladder first so everyone could look up my skirt. And they weren't joking!

"I've had some tough situations and I've learned to have a bit of a sense of humor. But also to draw the line and don't let things go too far.

"For example, when I first came into Pacific Bell, one of my peers kept calling me 'honey.' I have no idea what possessed him to do this. So every time he would call me honey, I would respond and call him 'sweetie pie' or 'muffin cakes,' until finally everyone was laughing so much at him that he just stopped. These were in public meetings. He would say, 'Oh, excuse me, honey, could you please. . .' and I would say, 'Sure, muffin cakes!' It didn't take him that long to get it.

"I found that a sense of humor is an effective weapon. If you're in a very serious situation, then definitely skip the humor and go right for a very direct approach. But I have found in changing a culture, where people many times are unconscious of their behavior, taking a humor route so they realize what they're doing, in a non-threatening context, is going to be is a lot more effective."

How do you influence people to your way of thinking?

"Not always successfully, I will have to say. But one of the approaches I have found to be effective is to think about what's in it for them. I certainly didn't invent that approach--it's very common in sales--but I do think that there are many opportunities

for both parties to win, whether it's in negotiation with a vendor or with a customer. In my current role, I have a lot of conversations with Wall Street and with the press. Helping people to see why an issue is important to them, why it's interesting, why it's compelling and putting yourself in the other person's shoes is probably the one thing I feel can be very effective."

Someone heading a company or holding an officer position has a lot of power. Yet there are women holding these types of positions who don't feel that power or don't recognize that power. How do you deal with the power that comes with your position?

"You said a key word and that is recognition. I have observed a number of women in my career who hadn't realized that the power comes from the position and not from them personally. I'm sure we've all seen people who were in a job and all these doors opened to them. Corporate America runs by position. If you're in the CEO chair, there are expectations of you, there are things that people offer to you, there are opportunities for different kinds of communications, all kinds of opportunities. As soon as you're out of that position and you're not working, the same opportunities for that position will go to the next guy sitting in that chair. The good news about that is that all the power is there to be stepped into it. It's simply a matter of stepping into it because it's there with the position. It's very important for women to realize that and fully step into the senior executive roles with all of the expectations and the opportunities that come with that. You get the job and you're expected to perform. Stepping into it and fully understanding the opportunity is the most important thing."

There are comments made that women who hold these positions act very much like men. What are your thoughts on that?

"That's true to some extent, just as, for example, women basketball players act very much like male basketball players. I just saw two basketball games over the weekend on television. One was a male professional team and one was a female professional team and I found myself thinking, gosh, they look a lot alike. There's no reason that women should play the corporate game radically different from men, because it is a game. There are rules, there are positions to play, there are expectations, just like in a sports game. You would fully expect for behaviors to be very similar. I do think many of our cultural expectations of women are very different than they are for men. But I don't believe that there's any reason to think that women shouldn't act very much like men when they're playing a particular position which would call for those types of behaviors."

It's using more of that masculine side of your personality versus that feminine side?

"All individuals have a mix of masculine and feminine sides, whether you're male or female. Many men have a very well-developed feminine side and vice versa for women.

"I believe just as men use their more masculine sides, if you will, in corporate America, women do as well. And vice versa, when you're playing with the kids, men use their more feminine side and women do as well. It's much more about masculine and feminine tendencies than it is gender-determined.

"There does seem to be a value judgment about modes of behavior in corporate America. The value judgments come from the last 50 years of cultural norms that have developed in the United States."

Why do you think there aren't more women officers, especially with profit-and-loss responsibility?

"I would say it's a factor of a couple of things. One is time; women have not dedicated themselves full-time to a career for as long as men have. It's a matter of education. It's only been in the last 10 or so years that women have made up an equal number in MBA courses in the United States, which is the prime training ground for business. A phenomenon in the last five years or so is the Internet that is largely gender-blind and based on results. Many more opportunities have been created. Women are founding more companies too, which means you can become CEO by declaring yourself one."

How do you break through to that level? Any suggestions?

"I believe that performing to the best of your ability maximizes your chances of success within a company culture. I've made a number of choices in my career out of the four or five job moves from different companies I have made in the last 20 years. I've made two of those moves specifically because I felt that the culture wasn't a fit in terms of it leaning towards giving men more opportunities. One was at Chevron, my first job out of business school where I wasn't a man and I wasn't a chemical engineer and I was told directly I wouldn't get to the executive suite. They were very up front about it, which is now illegal. They've had a lot of problems with that. I looked around and I didn't see any women at the top and within the space of four years or so had pretty much topped out in my mid-20's, which I thought was ridiculous. And so I decided to leave. It was very clear.

"At SBC, it was a lot more subtle, certainly, but I just didn't fit. There are so many opportunities out there and it is such a wonderful time in business that there's really no reason to bang your head against the wall. Do the best you can, try to maximize your opportunities for success within a company. But if you really feel the culture isn't a fit, it's time to move on."

Would you do anything differently?

"I don't hang on to a lot of regrets. Each step and each experience in our lives helps to bring us to the next one. For example, had I not left SBC and gone to US West I wouldn't be at NorthPoint today. Each event in our lives and each experience that we have helps us get to the next one. The important thing is to learn from them and go from there."

"You must reevaluate, reassess and constantly reformulate along the way."

MARY FARRELL

- **Managing Director, Senior Investment Analyst and Member of the Policy Committee for PaineWebber, Inc.**
- **Degrees: Bachelor of Science - Economics**
                  Master of Business Administration - Finance
- **Children: 2**
- **Age: 50**

Mary Farrell is often quoted in leading publications, seen
on national television, and is also helping other women
through lectures on the topic of women and investing.
Ms. Farrell is a regular panelist on *Wall $treet Week with Louis
Rukeyser*. She has written a book called *Beyond the Basics: How
to Invest Your Money Now That You Know a Thing or Two*.

Along our journey in life, we each have to decide, for ourselves,
what is most important to us and understand the consequences of
the decisions and choices we make. For Mary, having a family
was a priority in her life. She decided at the beginning of her
career that she was going to balance her life to have children,
spend time with them, and raise them the way she wanted to. She
understood and took responsibility for the impact that choice had
on her career.

How would you define success?

"You really have to define it very individually, because it's only
your goals and your own constraints that determine what success
means for you. Particularly if you're talking to women, family is
an issue. I realized early on that I wanted to be successful, but I
also wanted to have a family. That greatly impacted how I was
going to define success for myself. That's important even today--
for women to be very realistic about what they're willing to do and
what they want to do to achieve that crucial balance in life."

What decisions do you make to bring balance into your life?

"I realized early on that for me, success was going to include a
balanced life. I knew that I wanted to be successful in the
corporate world, but I also wanted to be a wife and mother. I
always, in the beginning, planned to make those two work in

escalates. Instead of getting easier, as I once thought, it does get harder.

"A crucial issue is control over time, and my choice of a particular job reflected that. There are some jobs that do not give you control over your time, and these are obviously difficult for mothers. I went into the equity research department, knowing that research was something that could be done far more flexibly than many other jobs. Obviously, you have to respond to clients, changes in the market or changes in the companies that you're following, but it doesn't matter whether that work is done at home after the kids are in bed from eight to midnight. You can walk out of the office at five, you just get it done at another time."

How do you fit in going to activities with your children?

"I actually worked at several firms before I landed at a firm that was open to the kind of flexibility that I needed. That was not an accident. That was part of my career goal and I was very fortunate because I worked for someone who was very bottom-line oriented. As long as the work was done, my boss didn't care if I went to the school play, and I managed to make it to a lot of them. It took a lot out of me to make up work at the end of the day, but of course, it was very important to me to be able to do that. You can't always, but when you set your priorities and look at the big picture, it's a lot easier to fit it all in place."

Is there a specific success formula that has enabled you to reach the top?

"I thought there was a formula when I started out. I found out you must reevaluate, reassess and constantly reformulate along the way. I'd note that now with technology and the Internet, things are changing so much more rapidly that you have to constantly change and respond to the changes and the environment around you. Whereas technology is definitely a friend to the extent that it has given us a lot more flexibility, such as telecommuting and the ability to work with your computer on your own time, it also accelerates change, which can present difficulties and challenges."

What are those "unwritten rules" you were able to uncover that allowed you to rise so rapidly and be successful?

"That is the crucial question because there are so many unwritten rules. Most women from my era went to school but weren't expected to go into the job market on a career path.

"The sole career advice I got was, 'Get your teaching certificate in case, God forbid, you should ever have to support yourself.' There was a lot I didn't know and it was exacerbated in my situation because I went into a man's business. Going in as a professional to the financial industry, I was virtually always surrounded by men, rather than women. There were no role models; I had to make my own way. One of the unwritten rules is that you can't expect the environment to change for you. Rough language on the trading floor was a given in that era. It was foolish to be upset about it. Or if you wanted to get invited out for a beer with the guys, you had to listen to the raunchy jokes. I learned early on that I had to fit in a certain environment, but of course, that was the 70's. Things have changed a great deal in the 80's and 90's. But I use it as an illustration because people should be focused and overlook the shorter term inconveniences or nuances that may not be perfect. It is important to understand that you have to be part of a team. You must be a team player. There are very few jobs in this world where you can make it on your own. You need the support that comes from a team. Even more so, with technology and with rapid communications, you have to be adaptable and able to work with a wide variety of people.

"Interpersonal skills are very important. I remember reading a business school study of people who were fired, and the common denominator was their not getting along with other people. You spend a minimum of eight hours a day at the office with your colleagues. This is in essence your second family. In fact, many spend more time with that second family than with their nuclear family. Getting along with people is crucially important and very helpful in a career.

"I have to admit to taking a shortcut. Where you found most of the successful women on Wall Street in the 70's and 80's was in research or sales and the reason was that there is a measurable bottom-line. I think it may still be difficult for women who are in corporate finance or in a corporation management hierarchy. To some extent, I realized early on that if that you were recommending companies that made money for clients, those clients didn't care whether you were male or female or from Mars, they were happy to support your career. That was really why I chose research. I strategized by initially going into a group that had very little competition--emerging growth companies back in the 70's--figuring I would stand out and be more visible much sooner than if I had gotten into the drug industry, for example.

"When you rely on more subjective measures, some difficulties can kick in. Of course, it's never quite as simple as *just* the bottom line. But that's where some of the other things that we talked about come in: interpersonal skills, adaptability and recognizing and meeting the needs of clients. The brokerage industry and financial services are heavily client-based businesses, and to the extent that you're good at what you do and deliver that to clients effectively, it goes a long way towards assuring that you're going to get noticed and get promoted. When you're the only woman in a department of 35 professionals, and they rate everybody's performance, you want to be right up there at the top and you're going to get noticed if you are.

"Additionally, you should be very passionate about what you're doing. I was very fortunate; I majored in economics and finance and I love the stock market. I love economic research and strategy, so it makes creating a successful career a lot more palatable. In fact, a study was done at Columbia University that compared men and women business school graduates. It looked at the women who had left the labor force and those who stayed in the labor force. The constraint for the women who left wasn't whether they had children or were married, it was whether they liked their jobs. The ones who were happy with their jobs somehow managed to combine work and home life successfully, be it a family or a husband or whatever. I feel that way about my job, and that I am very lucky that I found the work I love."

Tell me more about how your mind thinks. How did you know you should go into research?

"Right now, I'm an investment strategist, and strategizing is something that has always come naturally to me. I'm very analytical, and out of the analysis comes strategizing. For example, I strategized my career. Sometimes it took a lot longer than I anticipated. Occasionally, people have said to me, 'Oh, you were so lucky that you got on *Wall Street Week with Louis Rukeyser*.' Luck had nothing to do with it.

"I started early on writing articles for trade publications even though I didn't get paid for that, because it was a way of gaining visibility within the industry. Along the same line, I accepted speaking engagements because that put me in front of senior people in the industry, which was also a strategy. Performance is not enough; I knew that I would need more, so I went about very methodically obtaining greater exposure to much more senior people outside the firm which I then could bring back within the firm to help to my career."

How have you changed as you've come up the corporate ladder?

"I still remember the days when you would go to a meeting and it would be at a club that didn't allow women: I'd have to go up the back stairs, and once I was led through the basement kitchen to get upstairs. But, those days are behind us. I am really very grateful now that the environment is not just hospitable towards women, but actively welcoming women. I no longer feel like the odd person out.

"I feel very good about having reached a certain level. It's been a long struggle and a challenge along the way. I feel good about where I am now."

You are in an environment that is so male-dominated. How did you figure out how to fit in and did you change at all in that environment?

"I have one big advantage: I grew up with three brothers and there were six children born in seven years. We're all very close in age. I dealt with boys all my life and we were all very competitive. I swam competitively for eight years growing up and played Monopoly games at home which would go on for days, if not weeks. Being in a competitive environment wasn't something that threw me. But, the first decade of my career, I struggled a lot about how much I should change. I wanted to be a part of the team, but not necessarily one of the boys. I felt a lot more confidence in the second decade of my career and crucially, I realized early on that I could only be who I was. I am not as tough as one theoretically should be on Wall Street. I was brought up to be a nice person. I tend to, in my dealings with others, be empathetic or sympathetic, and people I work for have told me that I need to be tougher.

"On some level, I have been. But in answer to your question, I knew there were certain things I couldn't change. I could never be as nasty as some people think you need to be. It may have taken me longer, but it paid off because I'm still myself. Twenty-nine years later on Wall Street, I'm still pretty much the same person I was in 1971."

What is your greatest success?

"My greatest success was when Louis Rukeyser asked me to guest host one night in his absence. I was the first woman asked to do that. But I was about as close to panic as you could possibly be. The producer was wonderfully encouraging and helpful, and the entire staff could not have been more supportive. I knew I had a half-hour of live television with a guest, and I found out that night that asking questions is a lot harder than answering them. I remember telling myself, 'You can do this, you can do this.' Then as we got closer to the airtime, I reversed it: 'You can't make a fool of yourself. You can't fail.' The fact that I got through that half-hour was to me the biggest challenge I had ever faced. I would say it came out as a success that I'm very happy the producer was pleased with."

What is it like to know that all these people are listening to you? Not only do they listen to you, but they're taking your advice, and you realize you have such an impact on people.

"It's a heavy responsibility. I would say I'm very fortunate at PaineWebber because I work as part of the investment strategy group and we have always been very focused on the fact that we're strategizing for real people out there, about real money. We may be doing research but it's not in an ivory tower. We realize if we are not successful, our clients are not. I have had so many experiences out in the field where clients come up to me after a seminar to thank me and say, 'Oh, we took your advice ten years ago.' I get enough of that feedback to realize how crucially important it is. I'll tell you, we have not been right 100% of the time. And we suffer a lot. It is not a paper loss to us, it's very real. I take my job as an extremely serious responsibility."

What is another defining moment in your life?

"Defining moments for me have been defeats. There's a misconception out there that if people are successful, they've had an easy way up the corporate ladder. But for me, really, success comes from overcoming defeats, from the fact that you made mistakes, or you didn't get that promotion, or you didn't get the recognition, and instead of getting upset about it or turning off, you worked even harder. I know people who have left the industry or left jobs because they didn't feel they were recognized. I always viewed those situations as temporary setbacks. It just made me even more determined, and I would step up to the challenge. I viewed any setback or defeat as a challenge. That you picked yourself up after a defeat was the important thing."

Were there specific situations where you felt you were experiencing some resistance? How did you get around it?

"It certainly has not been a straight-line trajectory. I have been stopped off at many points and what I've tried to do is be very honest and objective with myself about that. Sometimes I see women viewing any career stall as a glass ceiling or a form of discrimination. In my case, oftentimes I was able to really be objective to realize that, for example, when my children were young and took up a lot more time, that perhaps I shouldn't be advanced at this stage in my career for my efforts. Maybe this was a career plateau that was quite appropriate for my emotional energy level. I was always very careful to do a more-than-adequate job, but to earn a promotion you need to go way beyond that. I tried to be brutally honest with myself about what was interfering with my advancement.

"Having said that, I did change jobs on two occasions because I really felt I had not been rewarded. I was not going to be able to further my career under certain circumstances. You have to look internally and make sure it is not you. But there are truly times when you may be in an environment that is not conducive to achieving your goals, and as difficult as it may be, you take a deep breath and step back to the plate and make a career move.

"If you have serious long-term goals, as long as you're sure you've given it enough time to achieve them, then it is inevitable that you must move on."

We all make sacrifices in life, depending on what we want. What kind of sacrifices have you made to reach this level?

"I have no life, other than my work and my children and my husband. In fact, the only friends I really can have are friends who work and understand that. I have a very dear friend who refers to me as her best friend. We talk once a year and we've been friends for almost 30 years. We just recognize there will be a time in our life when we can come together. When my children were young, the only socializing I did was with other parents of young kids and we would do potluck suppers and brunches, but there just is not a lot time in my life for other interests. I was once asked on a program, what are your hobbies? I was embarrassed. I don't have any. Reading the *Wall Street Journal* doesn't sound like much of a hobby. Other than reading, I simply don't have any time for hobbies.

"I have a home up at the shore near the town where I grew up and I am trying to redecorate it because I realize that after 15 years, I have still just moved in. Again, spending time on those things is not time I have to spend. I feel in retirement I can do all these things I've saved up for 45 years. But the decision to have children and work, and I don't mean to suggest this is what other people have to do, has meant cutting out virtually everything else."

Do you play golf?

"No. I did before my first child was born. But I quickly learned that one does not spend Saturdays golfing when you have young children waiting at home."

When you go into a meeting, there must be times when you're the only woman. What's the impact of that? It seems like men act differently when there is a woman in the room and women act differently when there's a man in the room.

"I do think there's always a different dynamic going on there and I tend to be shyer than a lot of men. I find men at meetings tend to talk very quickly and loudly, so I have to make sure I get my voice heard at meetings. But, I would have to be honest and reverse that and say that sometimes being the only woman can be a real advantage, and I am certainly not averse to using it as an advantage when it comes in handy."

Like what?

"I'm just thinking, of course this is different today, but back in the 70's, I was one of the few female analysts, and companies used to like that. You'd be in a group, and because you were the only woman present you would always be seated to the right of the chairman or the president, the most important person there, because that's what etiquette says. This would be a tremendous opportunity to get to ask more questions and more importantly, you tended to be remembered. If they met over the course of the year, two dozen analysts and you were the only woman, they tended to remember you, and I tended to be friendly and outgoing to these people and would have my phone calls returned first. I knew that because they would say, 'Oh, I had all these phone messages. I called you first.' Thank you!

"I used it to establish relationships that really paid off in a business sense. I didn't mind doing that."

What other advantages do you think women bring to the workplace?

"Women are innately well-organized; they have to be. They tend to find themselves in situations where they have to be quite well-organized. When I come to the workplace, I always approach my jobs with the same way I approach my life--analyze, strategize, and get the job done. Just to give an example, I used to work as late as all the men before I had my first child, and I remember after the baby was born, I would make a point of walking out at five. I found that just made me reorganize my day a lot better. When you thought you could stay till eight, you kind of let things go. When you knew you were leaving at five you became far more productive. I think that is something that women tend to be very good at."

Nobody said anything or thought something different of you because you were leaving at five?

"That's why I changed jobs and went to a firm that was bottom-line oriented. When I went to PaineWebber, the director of research was a woman with two children and she understood perfectly. She is now president of a money management organization; she's the first woman to run a capital markets group on Wall Street--and she was doing it with two children. She recognized the constraints, but she also knew that this job could be done as long as you had the flexibility."

There still seems to be the perception that if you're of childbearing age, and you're thinking about children, that you're going to take off time, and therefore there is some hesitation to put you on the path.

"There are always going to be jobs that are very difficult to combine. When you deal with the stock market and you're dealing with clients' money, you can't disappear for three months. Therefore, women have to be realistic in their career choices. Many more companies are offering flexible options, and are now pursuing women employees as a long-term investment. In fact, when someone quits it generally takes more than three months to go through the process of interviewing, replacing and getting the new person on board. Given the low unemployment rate, companies would rather opt for, 'You can have your three months; we just want you to come back.'"

Have you had mentors in your career?

"Unfortunately, in the beginning, there were so few senior women on Wall Street, I certainly never found one. But, I was very fortunate in two: one was the woman who hired me at PaineWebber, a very successful woman, extremely smart, very personable, tough where she had to be, but a wonderful human being. Just watching that she could do it was incredible. She has been extremely supportive of me while I have been at PaineWebber, both personally and professionally. Also, my second mentor is the head of our strategy group, whom I work with on the Investment Policy Committee. Just by observing him, I've learned a lot--he's absolutely brilliant and has been a great teacher. I remember the first year I was working for him, which happened to be the year of the stock market crash. I learned more in that one year, working with him, than I learned in the prior 15. He has also added to my job satisfaction--having that constant intellectual challenge.

"One thing that I feel very good about is that so many of the women I have hired and who have worked for me have gone on to do major, bigger, better things, and I'd like to think that I helped them along with some mentoring. I view that as a source of enormous satisfaction: to see somebody that you feel you nurtured and helped along, running with it and using it to their advantage."

Have you had role models in your life? What did you learn from them?

"That goes back to my family because they really were devoted to very hard work and were very motivated. Our family activity was going to the library every Wednesday night, so we probably sound like a bunch of nerds, which I'm sure we were. But, we were expected to always do well in school, always work, and we all contributed a great deal to putting ourselves through college and graduate school. I feel enormously fortunate that I had a family who prized academic success and then professional success as well. That was probably one of the best starts I could have had and that pretty much stayed with me. In fact, because I've worked all my life and I come from a family where everybody worked, I almost don't know what I would do if I didn't work. I guess that gets back to why I have no hobbies."

What have been your biggest challenges, other than the man/woman challenge when you first started out?

"Managing time and doing the right thing, considering I have two children, has really been very challenging. I've never been able to fully separate business and personal because they've always been competing parts of my life that had to be dealt with simultaneously. That's been a real challenge. It was a challenge in many ways to be in a man's world. To make myself function in a world that was quite different from what I had known, and also to find my own way, was a challenge. I wish, in retrospect, there had been a lot more senior women that I could have looked to along the way.

"I will say, though, I don't want to make it sound like I'm taking too much credit. I was very fortunate because about the time I went to Wall Street in 1971, there was starting to be a group of women--not many of us, usually just one or two at each firm. Interestingly enough, almost 30 years later I am still very close friends with many of those women I met in the early 70's. None of us mentored each other, but we provided a very strong support network for each other all these years. I sometimes think that in many ways, if you didn't have mentors, having a network of women was certainly the next best thing because there was always someone you could call and really get some important input. That has been a major boost in terms of the support that wasn't there through the traditional network that the men had, but we created our own."

What is one thing that makes you different from others that has allowed you to gain this type of leadership role?

"I'm persistent and ambitious and always have been that way. I think persistence is very important. No career goes straight up. Sometimes you have to realize it's not you. There are factors that you have no control over environmentally, in terms either of the economy or of your own business. You may be in a business that happens to be out of favor at that time.

"You have to recognize that there are going to be times when you must be patient. But it's that persistence that pays off. Constantly building your skills helps as well. I do have an MBA, but my technology skills, because I got my MBA so long ago, were nonexistent. I've had to constantly reinvent and educate myself and expand. Again, getting back to how rapidly the Internet and technology are changing, that education is important.

"But finally, being ambitious has certainly helped because it kept me from taking no for an answer. 'Okay, you don't think I'm good enough; well, I'll just prove it.' It worked for me."

You are in a very powerful position. How do you use the power that comes with your position?

"This is going to sound corny and self-serving, but I try to use it for good."

How do you do that?

"Years ago, I told PaineWebber that we should be educating women clients. I could see this among my friends. They were in their 30's. They had good jobs. They were making money and they didn't know how to invest and in my era, nobody brought up daughters to think they needed to care about balancing a checkbook, never mind investing or taking control of their finances. In my era, you were brought up to believe your husband would take care of you. I felt we should really be doing investor education programs for women. Initially, there was some skepticism: 'Why are we doing this? How does the firm make money on this?' They finally supported me. We held seminars telling women what they had to do, why they needed to plan for retirement, and I really got the firm to do many good things like that over the years. Also, some of the organizations I have been involved in are non-profits; talking to the firm about supporting them, that's a good use of power."

How do you influence people to your way of thinking?

"I try to be nice about it and again analytical--and show them how it works for them. Only when you convince them that we both benefit, that this is a worthwhile goal, but it also is good for business--that's the most effective way to do it. You have to persuade them that everyone wins in order to get things accomplished. It's a lot easier when you can."

Some women say they don't feel valued, listened to or respected in the business world. What advice would you give?

"You really have to produce the performance; you have to be a team player and you have to be circumspect about understanding what the rules of the game are, so that you're playing by those rules. Women can have self-defeating behavior by refusing to understand the rules or to play by them. I have to say I have a hard time answering that because I feel like I have always been listened to in my environment. I feel like I have always been given opportunities over time. Not necessarily as soon as I thought I should get them, but I found that by really trying to be the best possible employee, I really didn't experience a lot of those problems."

What kind of rules?

"Again, in the research department, I knew there was one rule. Your stocks have to go up. It's simple as that. I remember talking to a young woman who was concerned about this, that, and the other thing, and saying to her, you need to be concerned about one thing and one thing only--your performance. Don't care about what's happening over there. Don't care if you think this is being mismanaged there, because the bottom line is, that's not how you're going to be judged. You're going to be judged on one thing and one thing only and if you've got that down pat, then maybe you can worry about accusing people about mismanagement or anything else. That is irrelevant to your career progression and sometimes, at the risk of oversimplifying, you just have to do your job the best you can.

"Everyone has to be very careful about the environment that they pick. You have to be realistic. It's far easier to be successful in a growing area. That was again part of my strategy, to go into an environment that showed strong growth, because it would be easier to grow with it than to go against the grain."

Has there ever been a time when you wanted to give up?

"Yes, there have been a lot of those times. It does get very overwhelming. It's hard when you're traveling and balancing family and trying to get the job done. Sometimes, it does seem so overwhelming that you just want to put your head in the sand, because you think, 'I can't possibly get this all done.' But you try to get through that as quickly as possible."

How do you get through it?

"I make lists. And then I feel better. I have several different categories of lists that I put down and somehow, for me, when it's on the list it's out of my head, and sometimes I don't worry about it as much. Then it's a matter of methodically going down the list and getting as many things done one at a time as you can.

"Actually, I carry a notebook at all times and I'm constantly writing down stuff that needs to be done for any part of my life.

"I need to bring up a point which needs to be brought home to a lot of people: today's retirees are the last generation that is going to have the Social Security and Medicare combined with life-time pensions and health care benefits that retirees have typically gotten. Most companies are getting out of the pension business, many aren't giving those life-time health care benefits and certainly it is clear that many of us won't even get the Social Security and Medicare of today, either. If baby-boomers don't prepare for their retirement, they're going to be in trouble."

Do you have any regrets?

"I guess in some ways I regret that I couldn't clone myself and do everything. But I was very fortunate; I had a working mother so I don't spend a lot of time feeling guilty about being in the work force. Sometimes it would have been nice to do some of those things, like baking cookies with the kids, instead of buying the Christmas cookies. But we did do a lot of things, especially when they were younger. Also, one regret--sometimes people look at me and say, 'Look at how successful you are,' and I look at what I might have been if I hadn't had children. Not that I regret the constraint, my kids have been a major factor in my life, but I could never do global travel. I just made a decision years ago that my travel would be extremely limited even now.

"In fact, when my daughter left for college, one of the senior people at our firm said, 'Didn't your daughter go to college? Now you can travel more.' I said, 'No, I still have one son at home.' He wrote down on his calendar when my son would be leaving for college. The firm has been very supportive all these years, but I have taken a hard line--I don't travel globally. I won't leave my children for extended lengths of time, and even my domestic travel is put into very small time frames so I will not be away from the kids for too long. It certainly hurt my career and I understand that and I accept that. I think it's fair. I didn't expect that I could announce I would not be competitive across the board and that it would be overlooked. That has certainly hurt my career, but I would not put it in the category of a regret, because again I was going for balance, and I got it.

"It's truly a career that has taken a lot of directions I never could have anticipated. But it certainly has been fun on the way."

What's next?

"I'm kind of fascinated by that because my son does leave for college in a year and a half, and I'm wondering, like, when I actually have some time, maybe I'll find out that I was using the children as an excuse all these years--for having an undecorated house, and not entertaining, or not playing golf. I have heard from friends who are a little bit ahead of me on this, that you can re-energize. You re-energize and refocus and really rethink. I love the stock market; I love investment strategies. I don't think I will be doing anything too different, but maybe I'll finally do some global travel."

"One of the things that has made me successful over time and not only in work but in most of my dealings, is that pretty consistently, what you see is who I am."

URSULA BURNS

- **Senior Corporate Vice President and Vice President Worldwide Manufacturing Operations at Xerox Corporation**
- **Degrees: Bachelor of Science**
               Master of Science – Mechanical Engineering
- **Children: 2**
- **Age: 41**

Ursula Burns is responsible for manufacturing, corporate procurement, environmental health and safety, and supply chain operations at Xerox Corporation, Manufacturing Operations.

Ursula is a great example of someone who is comfortable with who she is and shows us that by being yourself you can reach the highest levels. Her clothing, hairstyle, and behaviors are unique to her and make a statement about who is. She learned to find a style that worked within her environment that has allowed her to excel.

What is success to you?

"There are three general segments. One is having a good idea of what you want in life, not only in work but in life. What kind of life do you want to live? How much time do you want to spend with your family, your friends? What kind of work is going to make you happy, and then what things are going to be in your life that fill your free time that make you you? Once you have defined that, success is being able to actually achieve those goals. It's not necessarily getting as far as you can in the company or making as much money as you can, but having a reasonable hold and grasp on what you want, what would make you happy--and then actually achieving it."

It's so great to hear about happiness, because sometimes when people define success, that is not what you hear from them.

"I had a narrow definition before. That's how I was before, until I became smarter."

What was that transition like?

"Time. I ran for a long time to get to where I wanted to be; I'm still not quite where I want to be. I found as I got closer and closer, as I made more and more money and got more and more accolades, that there were lots of things that had to do with my happiness and the feeling of being whole and complete, that had nothing to do at all with the place that I came to every day to go to work. Getting a good grasp on those things was important for me to feel successful at work and successful in life. So after a while, after you've headed in a single direction and gotten really close, you realize that there's only a little left to go--but if you got there, you still would need more to make you happy or to make you feel complete. Fortunately, I realized this a lot earlier than most people realize it.

"The biggest change for me happened when three big things came together. One was, I was married and living a childless, married life. Which is very different than a married life with children. My husband and I were having a great time. I had made some huge strides in my career. I went from working as the executive assistant to the chairman to working as a vice president and general manager of a business. I started to run a business and at the same time, I got pregnant. I realized then that I had to figure out how to focus my life a little differently than I was focusing it, which was, like I said, running really hard. We realized then that we had to change our life. I had to focus more on this family unit that we were creating, as well as on work, because I was still having a great time at work and loved work. But I had to figure out how to balance it a little better than I was.

"The big changing point for me was becoming pregnant and realizing that there was no way I could live the way I was living. Not if I wanted to raise my children in the way I wanted to raise them, the way I was raised."

Once you were pregnant and you realized you were going to have

to make changes, what choices and decisions did you make that allowed you to bring more balance into your life?

"One big one was having a huge discussion with my husband about what kind of life we wanted to lead and what kind of balance we would bring into the relationship from both sides. Without my husband, without the work and the life that he lives, there would be no way I could do all the things that make me successful. My jobs have required me to travel quite a bit. My husband had to, at that point, make decisions about what kind of work he was going to take, what kind of travel schedule he was going to have. Fortunately, his work--he's a researcher--allows that flexibility. We also had to make choices about where we were going to live. I had options to live in Connecticut at the time; a little bit later I had an option to live in England. We had to make some choices about who was going to follow whom, where. We were able to do that all, primarily because the time was right for both of us. We were able to balance very effectively how much time I could dedicate to work and how flexible he could be, which in turn allowed me to be flexible with the beginning - and end-of-day hours. It was working a partnership with my husband that worked out really well. And also having some people, friends and family members, who could help us when we needed the extra help in raising our kids."

How did you have to change as you were moving up the corporate ladder?

"I had to be more polished in how assertive I was. You have to learn how to read your audience a little bit better. The tolerance level when you're more junior in the company for deviant behavior is wider. It narrows significantly as you move up the corporate ladder. But, you can't fundamentally change your personality; I don't believe that that's possible. It's set when you're about five or six years old. You have to figure out a way to temper yourself to be effective without changing who you are. The thing that I have learned over time--and I have had some great teachers in this, not overt teachers, but covert teachers--is just from watching people. The big challenge for me is that I am a very out-front, assertive, quick-acting person, and you have to sometimes temper that so that people can listen to you effectively, so that they can actually take in what you're saying and act. Because you can't do everything yourself. You have to get people to follow you, follow your lead, and so you have to tailor your style to make it so that they can do that."

How do you get people to do things, influence others to your way of thinking?

"One of the things that has made me successful over time, not only in work but in most of my dealings, is that pretty consistently, what you see is who I am. There's not a lot of stuff that builds up around the edges, faces people have to peel away to understand what I mean and what my intentions are. I come across very well to people I've just met as being fairly genuine, and the good news is that as they get to know me, that feeling doesn't go away. One of the things I've learned is that if you can know your facts and you build up your opinions with some facts and data, as well as some emotional conviction, you can generally get people to listen to the basic story and direction. They can easily add on and build on and I'm more than willing to listen to any additional good news, good additions, and then we'll go forward. It's just being who you are and being willing to work toward getting the best end without a lot of ulterior motives. That's been the key for me in leading a big organization very effectively."

What would you say is a defining moment in your career?

"The biggest, the most defining moment--the moment is a long moment--was the year and a half that I worked for the chairman of the company, Paul Allaire--not primarily because he was the chairman, but because of the kind of person he is. He and I are so different in personality--I am a city person, up front, rambunctious, and he's low key, a very mellow kind of a guy, a very low blood-pressure individual. I had, up until then, modeled myself and pinned myself to individuals who were very much like me. The person I worked for directly before him was somebody who was like me. Unlike me in background, but very much like me in his approach to work: running very aggressively towards things and taking on lots and lots of different things, focusing on a broad spectrum. Paul showed me in that year and a half how it's possible to have a completely different personality than the person you work for and still be effective. And he showed me how it's possible to have a reasonable balance in your life and be effective. How it's possible to be a nice person.

"Up until then, I had moved pretty quickly in the company. Right before then, I was doubting whether I wanted to actually be what some of the people who were directly above me had become, which is interesting. They were people who spent so little time with their families, and whose travel schedules were insane. They basically had spouses at home who raised the kids. What they were doing was financially possible for me to do, but not emotionally possible. Paul showed me what was possible. It was great working for him because he actually helped to balance off the rough edges I had. That was a defining moment for me--working for him."

How did you get that job?

"When I joined the company I was an engineer working in a lab and through the years, my early years in the company, I had been seen by someone. His name was Wayland Hicks. We met in the hallway one day and got to talking and had a series of meetings about different subjects and he and I disagreed continuously. I didn't really understand who he was in the company. I didn't know he was as senior as he was and I would refute his statements and we would get into arguments. We actually became very good friends, just from different sides of the world. I mean, I'm a Democrat, African-American, city girl. He's a Republican, white male, country boy. That's a way to describe us. I got to know him, and he watched my career and would direct me to places, behind the scenes more than in front of the scenes. Little did I know he was doing some of the things that he was doing, like saying, 'Try her in this,' or, 'Keep an eye out for Ursula.' He moved to Connecticut to run all of our field operations. We had a tradition in the company, up until very recently, that the two or three top executives in the company had a top executive assistant. The assistants got a broad view of the company. The company got to see them in a different light and see whether these people were actually stars or worth the investment. He called me when he moved and asked me to move up to be his executive assistant.

"I had just married in October, and Wayland called me in November and wanted me to move in January, to be his executive assistant. After I gave it some thought, and my husband and I discussed it, I said sure. We can get back and forth on a plane. After about a year of working for Wayland, I got a call from him saying that Paul Allaire wanted to meet me the next morning and ask me about something. I knew what it was that he wanted me to do because his executive assistant at the time was moving and taking a job in Canada. I actually didn't want to do it (become his executive assistant) because I had been married by this time for a year and a couple of months and I had not yet lived in the house that I had been married into. It was time for me to go back home. Paul, at that time, had a very different personality from everyone else where I worked. I was not sure it would be in my best interest to take the position because I had proven myself in corporate and it was a big risk to go off and do another shift.

"He basically convinced me it was a really good idea that I do this, and I went to work for him. I had a personality that he had seen in meetings that was pretty forceful and inquiring. I asked a lot of questions about things that were happening and why things were happening. What he saw was a good balance between him and me--he was quiet and I was somebody who knew engineering and the development of the organization as well. It ended up being a great match. I stayed in the job for about a year and a half and then moved on."

It seemed like a good way to launch your career.

"It did. The executive assistant position launched your career, but your career was launched in the fact that you were considered for the executive assistant position. Because by the time you were considered for it, you were identified as someone who had a shot at being someone who would step out. There was a possibility that you'd crash, but at least you'd have a view, because there's 95,000 people in the company. So it was a good way to look and see."

You had a lot of exposure.

"Very high exposure. It's actually very high risk. If you screw up, it's public. You can't do anything dramatic. You can do some pretty embarrassing things to yourself, and to the person that you're supporting, if you're not careful. The personal risk is pretty high. It was relatively easy for me to find my way, figure my way through this and not screw up, even though some do."

What was your biggest challenge?

"My biggest challenge was when I moved to England. I took a job in 1995 running a business unit in the United Kingdom. The reason it was a challenge was three-fold. One, it was a completely different country and the practices in the United Kingdom are fundamentally different from the practices here, especially when it comes to the acceptance of women, the acceptance of women of color. It was hard for me to adjust to the fact that I was in a kind of Rome. I didn't necessarily want to do as the Romans do, but I couldn't very well go over there and change the whole culture over night. I would have spent all my time fighting--both inside and outside of work. That was a challenge.

"The other challenge was that most of my staff and the entire management of the company was not in England. They were here in the United States. I spent quite a bit of time communicating back and forth and developing a way to have a team, a management team, that was remote in time zones and distance from where I was.

"I also had to build a different relationship with my boss because I couldn't be there whenever he wanted me to be.

"Those three things were some of the biggest challenges for me, as well as to have some fun in the UK and to live a reasonably happy life. Also, to go to work every day and not spend all my time traveling back to the United States to have meetings. It worked out well."

What made you decide to take on such a huge task?

"I had been to the UK many times before and the idea of living in London outweighed all business risks and issues. It turns out to have been phenomenal. If somebody actually asked me to live there again, I would do it in a minute, in a second; we had the greatest time. Paul talked to me about this. Different cultures move along at different paces and clearly diversity in the UK is looked upon differently than it is here. He knew that there would be social issues outside of work issues, as well as work issues, but he said, 'If you want to go you're going to have to deal with those issues. You can't avoid them.'

"You have to be careful about the fights that you have, because you could be fighting every day. It's too much to fight every day, every confrontation, and so you end up basically picking the battles, picking the important ones."

Were there other times when being an African-American woman impacted your career?

"I can't imagine that being an African-American woman hasn't impacted my career. I went into a company, in a field, that there weren't a lot of women, much less African-American women. It impacts your career because you are the only one, or one of the very few, and you always are. It's not abnormal for me; it's probably more abnormal for people who see me. I'm very used to it. It's not clear to me how it impacts me directly, except that it does in every way. I'll use an example. I was watching a show the other day and they had three prominent African-American men in New York City. They were not from New York, but they happened to be in New York. They were talking about how difficult it is, how different it is to be an African-American male in society today. You walk into a store; people react differently to African-American men or women when they walk into a store than they do to the majority of men or women. When you try to get a cab, it's just different. When you say how did it impact my career, then we would be here forever, because that's who I am.

"The thing that I do and the thing that we as a community, the

African-American women at Xerox do, is to try to stick together and not to hide the difference. I am fundamentally different than a man; I am fundamentally different than a white woman. The way that we act--we have to make it so that we can survive, make it positive--is to actually point out the fact that we are different. All people have a common thread that we all have to live on. Those common threads we know and we can talk about. But you can't minimize the differences. African-Americans are almost always alone in meetings or in other corporate situations; it's very rare that you have anyone who looks like you. It's very rare that you find someone who has the same background that you have, who listens to the same music that you listen to. There are fundamental things about how you live that are different, and you don't try to make them go away. They will always be different and that's good."

Do you feel isolated?

"You feel alone a lot, but not necessarily isolated. No. Interesting choice of words. Alone, for sure, or different, unique, but not isolated. Isolation comes about, especially at work, if you actually can't build a network of people who can support you in getting your job done. I have a network of people I count on, white and black women, black and white men, who keep me going socially and at work. So I don't feel isolated. In meetings and in large groups, it's amazing that when you look at the group, you look out and say this is amazing, how consistently the groups are generally middle-aged, white men, still. Now, the middle-aged, white men are not bad, it's just middle-aged, white men."

How do you deal with that aloneness?

"You focus on what's important in getting your job done. My mother was a great model. I remember when I was trying to get into college, I said, 'Ma, very few people get into school.' And she said, 'Don't worry about everybody else, just worry about yourself. I mean, you can't worry about all these people who apply and don't get in; just worry about you applying and getting in.' You don't have to like everybody or necessarily be like everybody else or agree with everyone. You just have to get your job done.

"It's funny; I think that women can do this better than men can do this, and this is a generalization that might get me in trouble, but if you look at women, probably less so now than before, from the beginning of time, we've been taught to nurture and work in groups. You've always been handed something to take care of-- here's a baby, here's somebody to dress--so there is this natural ability to include--even if there's difference, you include them, nurture them--more than to compete. Now, there's always competition. I definitely compete, but the role of competition can be too absolute--winning at any cost. It's just fundamentally not there for me. More of a balance is there for me. Focus on what keeps you going, and what keeps you going is who you are and who you were raised to be, and not trying necessarily to be something else."

What prepared you to hold such a leadership role?

"My mother, no doubt. She died 17 years ago. Mother raised the three of us alone, with no help from anyone, and with focus and kindness. She had to be focused to have us survive. We grew up on the lower east side of Manhattan, in not necessarily a good neighborhood, but we had a great life. It wasn't like we were starving, nothing like that. She had an unbelievable focus to provide her kids a good life--we were poor, but we didn't really know it back then. It was a different life. Her focus was to have us be strong and successful in the future.

"She had a clear sense of what she thought we needed to succeed.

She let nothing get in her way, no confusion. No confusion about wanting to live in a different place. The place that we lived in was considered irrelevant to the problem. She didn't focus on trying to get another husband; that was irrelevant to the situation. It would have been better if we lived in a different place, that would have all been nice, but that was not reality. Her focus was to get us a great education, to have good selves and be centered, to have us have a really tight family and to just have a good grounding about what's right and wrong.

"The most money she ever made in her whole life was $4,400. We went to private school; my brother and sister went to Catholic school.   All three of us went to college; fortunately we got scholarships or state aid, because she would never have been able to pay for it. We were always clean. We didn't necessarily always have the best of anything.   There was a clear focus on what's important. If I can just be 50% as effective with all the resources I have--I mean, I'm rich compared to my mother. I have more. I have a husband. I have two kids instead of three kids. We have two cars.   We have a vacation home.   You name it.   We're focusing on, trying to keep a good set of kids. Trying to be good is hard, but it's possible.   My mother showed me that it was possible."

You stick to your values. There is no gray area--it's pretty black and white.

"That's right, pretty black and white. It's hard though. I tell you it's hard because values are cultural. Values are background based. This is where it's a struggle. This is where difference in the company, if not managed well, can be totally detrimental. My values are clear. They are based on how I was raised, who I was raised by, the environment I was raised in. I guarantee you that there are people as good in the soul, as good at work as I am, who have a completely different set of values, and were raised in a completely different way. That doesn't make them wrong or bad, it just makes them different. It has been difficult for me to understand that, but now I understand it. It's like a light went on. As you get older, you say, yes, who you are is as much where you came from and who raised you as what you are doing today.

"I can see why I think the way I think. I can also see how people who have a completely different background think the way they think. Being able to do that is important, and not make a judgment automatically as to if they are wrong or right. But to be able to be critical, have enough critical thinking skills to try to sort through what the motivations of people are."

What was your mind-set like to believe that you could come into a large corporation, like Xerox, and say, "I'd like to excel here"?

"I didn't look at it as a career, when I came to Xerox. When I finished school, I was pretty cocky. I decided I was going to be an engineer, because I had this knack for math, even though I wasn't trained very well while I was in school. I applied to a whole series of schools, and I applied to some away as well. I applied to schools that were close by to where I lived because I wanted to stay home, because we didn't have a lot of money, but also I liked my mother's cooking and it was really convenient.

"I went to a school and realized in the first semester that I was in trouble, because these people, who were my peers in this school, were very well trained. I mean, they were from some of the best schools, and here I was coming from Cathedral High School. I was in the first semester and I realized I needed a tutor in math. I had a tutor for a little while and then I realized, after interacting socially with my fellow students, that I had it all above these people. They had no concept about reality. Their whole life, outside of school, was their house. Basically that's what they knew. I had more knowledge about the real world than they ever did. I rode the trains, went all over the city, and saw things from a different point of view. That was an amazing advantage."

What were your key learning lessons?

"Number one, you have to be good at something. When it comes to work, people come to me and say, 'How did you do this? You've been an officer of the company since 1997; you were 36 years old.' You have to do something about which the company says yes, it's valuable, you're good at it. The company doesn't look at you and say I like the way this person looks, let's make him or her the head of manufacturing. You have to be good at something and you have to figure out what it is that your niche is going to be. It's not always what you studied, but whatever it is, you have to prove your excellence in that area, prove your value in that area. You have to be relatively broad as well. Having some idea of what other people go through is good, is solid.

"So you have to be good at something. A lot of people skip that step. They want to go straight to the I-want-to-be-vice-president stage, and I keep asking them vice president of what? What will we give you to do that you can give value to, that I know you can add value to? You have to be relatively good, and then you have to focus on action and excellence. It's not always--especially when you get to a big company--it's not always clear to people that they have to actually do anything, to actually have an output and a decision about which others can say yes, you did that. So action and excellence.

"You have to be good at your job. You have to be good at what you do, whatever it is that you started out doing, and branch out and become broad--if you want to get where I am. But not everybody has to get to where I am to be successful. This is a life about which I would interview ten people who are doing it before I chose to do it--you need to understand what you are choosing. Because it's not like people think. It's great, but it's hard."

There are people who feel like they're working so hard, but they don't get recognized for the work they're doing. How did you get recognized?

"I can't really hide very easily in a company, especially 20 years ago, when there were not a lot of me. So that was relatively easy. We also had a relatively astute company, from a diversity standpoint, so the company was looking for diverse people who had potential to be successful.

"The other thing is that I am not shy about having an opinion and making it clear what I think. I've learned over the years that it is best done with some facts and data. I'm not shy about telling people about what I think, about whether things are reasonable or not reasonable, whether things are above board or not above board, possible, not possible, and that is not common, not as common as you think.

"How do you step out? There's a core of a person that you are. You are either an analytical type of person, you're rambunctious, whatever. You have to make sure you're comfortable in that position, understand the basic building blocks of who you are. For me, it's relatively easy, so I speak up. But if you're in a meeting or in an environment where with your personality you would not naturally speak up, this is not something you do, then you have to figure out some other way: write, or get on special task forces where working in small groups makes you shine. You have to try to figure out a way to step out.

"Part of it is good preparation. I had not run manufacturing before, I had not even run a smaller plant before, but I had run large groups before; I had complex situations before. I had challenging positions with large budgets. The thing that I was missing here was the specific technical knowledge, but I also learn very quickly. So this is not a huge risk. The company doesn't sit there saying, 'Give this to Ursula.' How do they know that about me? They know because I have taken some time in the beginning to build a foundation where they can say, yes, she manages a large group and so on and so on. That's how you stand out: you have a great foundation to stand out on. You have to have something to stand on. You can't just hope people find you."

Were there times when you felt some resistance as you were working your way up the corporate ladder? How did you deal with that?

"Always. Most of the time, fortunately, it's from people who don't matter a whole lot to me. I don't really deal with them a whole lot. Resistance is always there. More because of my age, interestingly, than anything else. I've gotten pushed back about where I am or the groups that I'm leading or how could I possibly be doing this. Most of it has been because I was significantly younger than some of the people I was working with or who were working for me."

Did you ignore those comments, those reactions?

"No, it depends on where they came from and how they came. Sometimes, more often than not, I would be very clear about the fact that this is the fact of the relationship--for now, you work in this organization and I lead this organization. We have to figure out a way to work together."

You had a little heart-to-heart with them?

"Generally, especially if it's age-related. If it's race-related, I'm not generally that up front. This is a bias that I have. I think that race-related and gender issues are ingrained in people. I can have all kinds of conversations about how they should think, but it's not going to change a thing. Fortunately, this is not a problem with lots of people. But my way of addressing it or working with it is that there has to be a level of respect in the organization--upwards as well as downwards. As soon as that line is broken, that person won't be working in my organization any more. They have to do their job and have a basic respect for me as a person as well as me for them. If those two things are crossed, then we can't work together.

"The age issue, though, is one that I actually will face up to. It's like I said, gender and race, to me, are a little bit more insidious and harder to confront, harder to get results by confronting. It's harder to get results from confronting people, so I just try to manage them in a more professional way."

What would you say is your greatest success?

"Raising my children. They're turning out pretty well."

We all have to make sacrifices in our lives to get what we want. What sacrifices have you had to make to reach this level?

"The biggest sacrifice is my personal time. Every year for the last five years the start of my year has been to focus more on myself. And for about two weeks, I do it. I'm really good. I read books, I go out for a walk, with nobody around me. It takes two weeks, three weeks, then I'm back to spending a little more time than I wanted to at work. So, that backs up everything. By the time the end of the day comes, it's like 11:30 p.m. and it seems like I just started, and then what do I start? I start going through the mail.

At 1:00 a.m., I go to sleep and I wake up the next morning. It's just a cycle. It's gotten so big that I don't even know how I do it really. But now, one of the things my husband and I are going to do this year is we're going to take a vacation. I have a seven-year-old and an 11-year-old. We're going to take a vacation without the children. There has never been a time when my husband and I were both gone at the same time, except for once we went to the Olympics together.

"If I'm gone, he's home. If he's gone, I'm home. So, think about all the great places I've traveled to. I go to these great hotels, unbelievable hotels. I would call my husband and say, 'You would never believe how depressing this is.' I'd sit there and say to myself, 'You're alone, this is ridiculous.' So the one big sacrifice is the time to focus on me, just a relaxed focus. I still read a lot, but I would read three books a week, easily. Now, if I can get through three books a month that have nothing to do with work, I'm very happy.

"Sleep has not been a very big sacrifice. I guarantee you it's not going to be able to last forever, but I've never been a huge sleep person. I'm pretty good about sleeping in places other than bed. I don't sleep in meetings or anything, but I can take a nap in the car. I will do that because that's the way I can get my power level back up, my energy level back up. But I go to sleep at 12:30 a.m., 1:00 a.m., and wake up 5:30 or 6:00 a.m. I can do that for a while. I'm not necessarily proud of that fact; that just happens to be my metabolism today. I'm sure it will change."

I've read articles about women who are in your type of position and when they were asked about power, they commented that they don't feel powerful. What are your thoughts about the power that comes with your position?

"Oh, I'm definitely powerful. I definitely have a powerful position. There's no doubt about that. But I understand totally what they say about not feeling powerful. As high as you get, there is always somebody else above you. There's always somebody else there that can give you direction, who can pull your chain. The definition of power is control, right? Total control? When does that happen? I don't think there's a time when that happens. I have a powerful job, for sure. I'm a powerful person, but do I feel powerful? At work, I would say probably 10 to 20 percent of the time. It's not bad."

How do you deal with the fact that people are watching you all the time?

"I don't. It doesn't really bother me a whole lot. I don't have to deal with it, because it's natural, normal.

"I was walking in Wegman's (department store) and I was wearing what you wear when you don't think about what you're doing before you leave the house. This is what I do normally if I'm going to Wegman's, which is just throw on something so that I can get in and out quickly, and I wasn't thinking about it. I walked in and there were, in front of me, three people who were either peers or who had worked for me. I looked at myself and said to myself, 'This is how I look,' and then I thought about it, and I thought this isn't always how I look, it's who I am. I don't dress up to go to Wegman's. That's who I am. I go to the cafeteria. I buy what I buy, I sit down and it's who I am. More often now that I have been around for a long time. I'm just a regular person. I have lunch with the secretaries; I have lunch with whoever is around, whoever has an interesting conversation going.

"I analyzed Paul a lot, and one of the things that was clear was that when he became the CEO it didn't surprise him professionally, but he didn't make this big CEO adjustment. He just kept being who he was before he became a CEO. There are trimmings and trappings that come with it that definitely are positive, but he didn't fundamentally change a whole lot and that was good."

It's being comfortable with who you are. Understanding that people are going to have whatever perceptions they're going to have and not concerning yourself with it.

"That's right. There are not a lot of people in the world that I would want to be like. And this is a big deal. Sometimes there is a vision of what this person--me, my job--looks like. I can't find a person that I like a lot more than me. It's probably good being a black female--I can't find anybody who looks like me, so how would I even be like them? The only structural model that I have is me. I've gotten comments from people who say to me, 'I cannot believe your hair is natural.' This has been the most amazing thing to me. This is how I like my hair; it is not the standard hairdo. I love the way it looks and it's fine with me."

There are comments that women who reach these executive levels are very male-like in their behavior. How do you utilize your feminine and masculine side?

"Females are assertive or aggressive when they are protecting the things that are important to them. Probably more assertive than men are. I utilize my aggression--or my assertiveness--when I am defending things that are important to me. The values that I have, my family, the type of work I want to do, how I want the work done in my organization, the outputs I expect--I am very clear and fairly assertive about those things.

"There are 'masculine' traits about me. That has nothing to do with work. That has to do with how I was raised, what I like and my background. I like basketball; I like football. I will always, if you give me an option, walk around with short pants and sandals on. I will cut my hair relatively short. Those things are probably more 'masculine' than 'feminine.'"

It seems that some men don't like it if you're more masculine in your behavior.

"They sure don't like it."

How do you deal with that?

"Just like you deal with anybody who doesn't like the way you are. If you can't change it, you just persist. You've got to meter your approach. You've got to monitor how you interact with people, to deal with their personalities. But after that slight modification, all you can do is, simply, be who you are. People will say how do you deal with the fact that you're black. I don't deal with the fact that I'm black. It's a fact that I'm black. But other people have to deal with that."

Would you do anything differently?

"Have kids earlier--absolutely. If I would have known how much fun it was and how easy it is to actually work this out with the right support, I would have had more kids and had them earlier. I waited until I was 34 years old. I could have had three more kids if I did this well. I don't know if I would have been where I wanted to be in work, but it's possible to do this."

"You can have all the money in the world, a fold-out business card with all your titles, but if you don't have joy in your life, what's it for?"

SHELLEY BROADER

- Vice President Perishables Merchandising, Hannaford Brothers
- Degrees: Bachelor of Arts--Broadcast Journalism
    Bachelor of Science--Political Science
- Children: 1
- Age: 35

S helley Broader is responsible for over 150 stores in eight states under the names of Hannaford Food and Superstores, and Shop & Save.

Shelley is willing to take big risks and leap without being sure of what might be on the other side. She has such belief in herself that she knows that she will land on her feet and achieve her goals.

How would you define success?

"Happiness defines success and fulfillment. If you're happy in your life and you feel that you're moving forward, then you are successful."

What is your success formula that has enabled you to reach the top?

"I'm a risk taker. I have seen opportunities presented to me and taken advantage of them."

How have you taken advantage of them?

"When I graduated from college, most of my friends, my peer group at that time, were moving to Seattle and kind of extending the collegiate experience one more time and starting their careers there. I really took a different tack. I wanted to experience a part of the country that I had never been to, never knew about, and I just moved, with all my belongings, to Boston, with no job and no place to live.

"Basically, I just had my degree in hand and really shopped the market and looked to start my life there. That experience really spring-boarded my life."

What else is part of your success formula?

"Certainly, it's surrounding myself with the right people, hiring the right people, investing the time and training into the right people. As I move through my career, I try to bring people who support me through my career with me."

How do you know who the "right people" are?

"Certainly that's a hit-and-miss or trial-and-error proposition. I see people as a pie and everybody has pieces that are filled on their plate. It's being self-actualizing, really understanding what pieces of the pie you have on the plate and hiring people on your team who have different pieces than you have. One of the mistakes that a lot of people make is hiring in their own image. Then you've got a lot of people with the same shape pie in your organization and you really can't round out the full thought process. I've tried to look for people who can complement my strengths and weaknesses so we can build a whole team."

How did you have to change in your rise to the top?

"I really had to temper my enthusiasm. I have a tendency to be right up there. Very enthusiastic, very gung-ho, very aggressive. There are times when that can become overpowering. When you have a position, when you have a title that goes with that, you tend not to hear feedback any longer. I really had to temper my enthusiasm and in many ways my aggressiveness."

Have you had to deal with comments about being too assertive or aggressive?

"Sure. That's just a danger of management. You lose that ability to be self-actualized. I used to pride myself on really knowing my person and knowing my impact and being able to go into a room and really assess and read the room and understand my impact there. But as I've moved up, I've heard less and less, 'Oh, you should have said this,' or, 'It would have gone better if you had done that.' You can mistakenly interpret that to mean you're doing everything right, when, in fact, you're just not getting that feedback any more and that can lead to blind arrogance. You think you're doing everything terrifically well, when, in fact, it's just that no one is willing to give you feedback any longer."

What keeps people from giving you feedback?

"That has to do with positional power and maybe with personal power in some cases. You really have to find a peer group and find a support staff with whom you can have a relationship in which you can continue to get that feedback. No one wants to be naked in the board room."

Were there any particular events in your life that prepared you to hold this type of position?

"Yes, actually, my father passed away when I was about 13 years old. He was killed in a car accident. And I remember years later, my mother, sitting down with me--I was the youngest of four children--and saying to me that my life was going to be different from that of my brothers and sisters. My father wasn't going to be there to help pave the way for me and I really needed to do that for myself. When I say this to my mom now, she says she doesn't even remember that conversation. But that was just incredibly impactful to me, and I have always felt that I needed to make my own way in this world."

What are the major lessons that you've learned in life?

"Again, surrounding yourself with the right people. Certainly aligning yourself with the right organization and the right company. I have been fortunate to do that a few times in my career. I am certainly fortunate to do that now. Take advantage of training opportunities. Take advantage of cross-functional learning opportunities and really don't pigeonhole yourself with a single set of skills. I'm not practicing what I learned in college by any means, technically. Yet, I have a marketable set of skills and I can learn any tactical function. I can manage people and manage process. I can learn the tactical function that I'm managing."

How did you know when you were aligned with the right organization?

"It's like a friend. If you go to work every day and it's your job and you're anxious to get out of there every night, if it's not a place that you choose to be or people that you choose to converse with or activities that are engaging to you, it's not the right place. When you find the right company, it's engaging and exciting and innovative and it's motivating and you feel valued and you can add value."

Did you know going in that it was the right environment or was it going there and finding out afterwards?

"Always going there and finding out afterwards. I sometimes have a tendency to leap and hope there's a bottom.

"I left the banking industry. I was in investment banking. I worked for a regional brokerage firm and Hannaford Brothers was one of the clients. I went there, not based on the fact that I was just enamored with the supermarket industry. I went there based on the fact that in working with the people on a debt issuance at Hannaford, I felt that these were people I connected with. I liked their philosophy. I liked the way they did business. I liked the way they thought about their business and that's what lead me to Hannaford, not the grocery business but the environment of Hannaford."

What has been your greatest success?

"My greatest success is my family. It's my husband and my daughter. My daughter is 20 months old. Her name is Madison."

What was that like, having a child in the midst of your career desires to continue moving up the corporate ladder?

"It's a pretty welcoming environment at Hannaford. I had a very difficult pregnancy. I went into labor at 22 weeks, which isn't good. And spent basically from 22 weeks until my daughter was born, flat on my back. I could go downstairs once a week in our home to go to the doctor. That was my big outing."

Were you making business calls from bed?

"I did because I couldn't stand not to, but not because I was required to do so. My boss came to see me and he said, 'This is the most important thing that you need to do. Business will come and go, but this is a once-in-a-lifetime chance and you need to make sure you do what's right for yourself.'

"I ended up getting completely hard-wired in my bedroom, though. I had every gizmo known to man to stay in contact with the office. But it was really more for my own mental well-being than to run the business, because there are terrific people that work there that share that load."

What were your defining moments?

"Getting promoted or getting recognized within Hannaford Brothers has certainly been a defining moment for me. That moment of realization that I really can be a vice president or beyond, or senior vice president or president of a corporation. There's that moment when your boss tells you, 'This isn't the last job you're going to have; you're going to be my boss.' That's a pretty defining moment."

Were there times you felt resistance as you were moving up the corporate ladder? How did you handle that?

"Not in my current job, but that's why I've left positions in the past. When I realized that the effort wasn't worth the reward, and that I knew that my skill set would be appreciated elsewhere, I left."

At Hannaford, you spent a couple of years in various positions and all of a sudden hit a particular level and then escalated every year to a different job. What caused that to happen?

"I moved several times, physically moved. When I joined the company, I joined them in Albany, New York. I joined them at the ground level. I was a banker for them. I called them and asked them about employment. I said, 'I love your company; it's terrific. I have a lot to offer. I sell stocks and bonds. It's got to be like selling cans and hamburger. Is there a place for me there?' They basically said, right up front, 'We're aggressively looking for women, looking for women in management. We would love to have you interview, but you need to know that you're going to start at the register and then you're going to bag groceries and then you're going to work in the meat department and in the bakery department.' That made me want them even more, quite frankly.

"Because one thing that's terrific about Hannaford, and that I really learned to value about business, is understanding what makes the clock tick, understanding the cogs in the wheel. Certainly I pride myself on still being relatively in touch with the details and the tactics of the business. When I left banking, and joined Hannaford, I was at a pretty big supermarket in downtown Albany. I would be bagging groceries and see people come through that line that I had sat across the table from and signed multi-million dollar deals with. They probably ran home and called their attorneys, saying, 'She's at a register; she's on register seven now.'

"But, I really learned the value of understanding the business and starting at the bottom level. When you get that appreciation for the craft and for the business, you can only hope you make better decisions all the way up.

"Once I was in the stores, I was a store manager. I went into being a district manager shortly after that and then I moved to work in distribution. Once I was willing to move, my husband and I ended up moving to Maine, which is where our corporate headquarters are. That's when the series of the rapid progressions started, once I hit our home office."

How did you deal emotionally with what some people might consider to be a step-back in their career?

"It was a step-back financially and it certainly was a step-back status wise.

"I had a certain level of frustration where I was, too, which allowed me to deal with that better. In my previous job, I had a kind of series of revolving supervisors and it got to the point that I was pretty sure I wasn't going to become that supervisor. When I went in to talk about it, it became even more apparent. So, I was really ready and willing to go. At that point, I wanted to find a company that I could really have a career with and I was pretty tied to the Albany area. I looked at balance sheets. I had a banking background. I looked at a company that I could grow with. Hannaford had the balance sheet that would afford the luxury for me to grow. I knew that I would be making an initial sacrifice, but I also knew that I wasn't going to be doing those early chores for my entire career. I needed to do them to learn the business and to appreciate the business. If you're in retailing, it kind of gets into your blood sometimes, and you grow to love it, too."

We all have to make sacrifices in our life to get what we want. What kinds of sacrifices have you had to make to get where you are?

"Certainly, just working such incredibly long hours, incredibly long days, a lot of traveling, putting off starting my family a little bit. Just personal sacrifices, relationship-wise. I'm so devoted to my career. Lucky enough to have a husband that understands that, but when you have a single-minded focus for a lot of years, it can pigeon-hole you a little bit into a life that's pretty much focused on work."

What happened to allow you to bring more balance into your life? What types of decisions did you make or actions did you take?

"There are decisions that I made and some decisions that were made for me. My boss at the time that I was in retail in Albany really valued me and felt that I was nearing that burnout. You get so involved in what you're doing and I was just working continuously and he recognized the fact that I wasn't going to keep that pace up for a long period of time. Once you're in that cycle, you can no longer see that yourself. You almost need somebody else to point that out to you.

"There are people who are working 15-hour days, seven days a week, and they don't see a way out of it and they don't even know that they're in it. I was to that point, and he just pointed it out to me and said, 'You're killing yourself. You need to take a break. You need to do something different. You need to see a different side of the business.' Once I stepped out of that, I realized I wasn't utilizing my staff properly, I wasn't pacing myself and I wasn't as happy as I could be because I didn't have that balance in my life. I mean, under my watch, the task needs to get done, but it doesn't mean I need to do it. Some of that comes with maturity and experience."

If you were to look at your style, either about who you are or the way that you do things, what do you think makes you unique or different that has enabled you to climb the corporate ladder?

"My style is very direct. But I'm very collaborative, both within my peer group and with the people who work directly with me. I set expectations for them, but I don't need to guide people through every single step of the process. I like people to develop with me and develop their own plans and I don't want to be incredibly directive in the way that I lead. I want to create followership."

Is there anything else that you can think of that has made you successful?

"My desire to be successful. You have to follow through. You have to have the goods. You have to take the risk. But you can't just leap from risk to risk. You have to produce the results. I have a track record of producing the results."

What has been your biggest challenge?

"Balance is a huge challenge for me. I've been married for 11 years; it's terrific. I have a 20-month-old daughter, but it's difficult for me to regulate my life and to keep my life balanced. It's almost an arduous chore for me sometimes because I am so driven and I need to continue to work on that balance."

How do you deal with personal issues in your career life?

"I don't think this is an attribute--I probably think it's actually a flaw--but I really can compartmentalize. I just don't want to do that with my personal life, certainly, and having Madison is just a huge eye-opener and if that doesn't bring balance to your life, then nothing does. She's wonderful; I can't wait to get home and see her. Yet, when I'm sitting in a meeting and people are planning a travel schedule, I'm right in there planning that travel schedule, and it's not until I get back to my office that I realize, 'That puts me away 13 nights in a 26-night period; I can't do that.' But when I get in the moment, boy, I get going."

What role have mentors played in your career?

"They've played a huge role in my career. Specifically, at Hannaford Brothers, one of the people who hired me really took me under his wing and kind of sponsored me throughout the company. In my peer group, there are women who have a few more years of service with the company than I do, and I watch them progress and I watch them not change their person or not behave in a specific way because that's what was acceptable to get ahead. I mean, what you see is what you get and that's fine within our company, and seeing that allowed me real freedom there."

One of the statements people make is that some executive women act like men. How do you utilize both your masculine and your feminine side?

"I'm lucky to be born in the generation that I was born in. I don't think I would have been successful 20 years ago, because I really admire and really feel for the real trailblazers who tried to come up in Fortune 500 companies 20 years ago. They had to look in the mirror and say, 'I'm going to be more man than you'll ever be.' Probably more woman than they'll ever get, too. I don't think I could have done that. I have no desire to do that. If I felt that I had to change my personality and change my behavior and temper my person to be successful, I wouldn't be working for this company."

Have you had role models? What have you learned from them?

"My mother is a huge role model. After my father passed away, she hadn't worked in probably 20 years. She looked at her life and said, 'I've got three children left to go to school.' She was very young, in her early 40's, and she said, 'I've got my lifetime ahead of me and I need to do something for myself.' She went back to school and got a teaching degree and really started a life for herself. Very driven, very motivated and very supportive. That's a terrific role model: if you set your mind to something, you can really achieve anything that you want.

"My mother gave me this work of art. It's a little wooden sculpture of a woman flying with this crazy wirehair and stenciled on the bottom, it says, 'For a long time she flew only when she thought no one else was watching.'"

What are some of the "unwritten rules" you've uncovered that have made a difference in your being able to reach the top?

"I'm so bad at following rules; I have a hard time now with those. Women do have a particular challenge in that assertiveness and aggressiveness are interpreted differently in men than in women. Learning that is enough of a lesson or rule in understanding how to navigate or negotiate that issue in itself. Again, I have a hard time tempering myself so people see that side of me quite a bit at work."

It seems there are times when women are expected to act a particular way. How do you figure out when that rule applies and when it doesn't?

"Maybe I've been fortunate in my choices of employers and also in my own tolerance level. I am intolerant to that kind of double standard and when I've been faced with it in a different industry, I chose not to be in that industry any more. That's why I said I don't think I would have been successful 20 years ago. Because that was an absolute necessity. Now, you can find work environments that allow you to be the same person you are when you wake up in the morning, when you go to bed at night, and during your workday. That's where I choose to operate and I'm not really willing to temper my comments or my behavior or make sure that I'm not too girly or too emotional or too assertive. I'm not willing to do that any more."

In several articles written about powerful women, some of these women stated that they didn't feel powerful. What are your thoughts about the power that comes with your position?

"Positional power is tricky and it's difficult to understand. It's new to me and it's certainly something that I'm cognizant of, but whether I'm fully aware of it, I don't think so. That's why I mentioned it when we talked a little bit earlier about being self-actualized. You don't always get the kind of feedback you need, so you could be abusive of your power and not even know it. I would say that I don't feel the power.

"Some of that comes with time, some of that comes with the comfort level. I've been an officer in this company for around three years. Maybe that comes with time, too, but I don't feel any huge weight of that power. I see how power affects people and I see people who are unaware of their own power and effect change and don't even mean it. If I walk into the cafeteria and say, 'I hate macaroni and cheese,' that will be the last time it's ever served. People in power are unaware of that. I work hard on personal development, to try to keep that in check, and to understand power and understand my own effect on people and continue to try to grow my own repertoire of tools that I can use to manage and to lead. You're born with something, but the rest you cultivate a lot."

What types of things do you do for personal development?

"I do a lot of reading. I do a lot of watching. You can learn more from a good manager or a good leader. You can learn a lot from a poor leader. If you get enough things in your 'I'm never going to do that' bag, and in the 'I'm going to do that' bag, you can do all right."

How do you influence people to your way of thinking?

"I'm very enthusiastic about my beliefs. I don't give up very easily. I have a good knowledge of our business. When you couple some real enthusiasm about a goal or an end result with some solid business knowledge and a pretty tenacious way to do it, over time it influences people."

Has there been any time, as you've been working your way up, that you said, "I just want to give up"?

"Sure. There are times when something particularly frustrating occurs, maybe something that I was enthusiastic about and tenacious and really had an end in mind, and another path was chosen. It gets back to that balance question. Because of all the time, effort, and the energy that I put into my work, I get so emotionally involved. 'What am I doing that to myself for?' There are always those moments where you have kind of a gut check of what's going to make you happy, what's going to be best for your family. Everyone has those moments.

"You can have all the money in the world, a fold-out business card with all your titles, but if you don't have joy in your life, what's it for?"

Since corporations are male dominated, and men and women think differently, what type of skills have you used to be listened to, valued and respected?

"It's having an understanding of the business and being factual and having some business savvy in your comments. But I also think it's understanding your audience more than anything. It's changing and tempering your communication based on the receiver."

How do you figure that out?

"I'm very intuitive. I just do, I guess. That's something that I can do and that has provided me with some success."

It's relying upon that gut instinct when you're around people to be able to figure it out.

"What's important to them. How best to communicate my message to that group of receivers. Interjecting humor. Watching the verbiage. If I'm trying to communicate to a group of our store managers versus if I'm trying to communicate to Wall Street. Neither of those messages is going to play if you direct it to the wrong audience, so you need to be careful in how you go about that.

"It's management and it's understanding people and it's understanding the same message for one person may not ring true for someone else and it's that way with parenthood, I'm sure. Certainly, what works for my daughter may not work with another child. It's just varying your message and understanding that not everyone is responsive to the same stimuli. You might have to vary your stimuli a little bit. Mothers are professionals at that."

What drives you to want to go further and be more successful?

"It's internal. I'm not doing it for someone else. I'm doing it for myself. I'm capable of success and succeeding. I want to do it. I'm in the driver's seat."

As you look back, is there anything that you would do differently?

"I am the culmination of all my life experiences. There are certain things in my life that I could deem as mistakes, but if I didn't make them or didn't make that decision, I wouldn't have the knowledge base that I have now. When you ask me about regrets, sure there are things I wish I hadn't done, I wish I hadn't said, or job opportunities that came and went, but then I wouldn't be where I am today, doing what I am doing today. I wouldn't change anything."

Chapter 11

POWER PLAYS from the
Most Powerful Women

The women you have met have reached the top ranks of the corporate world. They have worked long and hard to learn how to influence people—below *and* above them—to achieve results. This chapter sums up the power plays that have allowed them to excel and to play with the big boys.

Typically, the MPW started at an entry-level job and mastered technical aspects of the work. Then they moved into managing the work of others. They became adept at building an organization and a winning team. To do so, they improved their communication, decision-making, and leadership skills, continually raising the performance bar. The majority of the women had advanced degrees, but most of their training was "on-the-job."

The higher they went the more polished they had to become both in how they presented themselves and their ideas. They were constantly reassessing their skills and what they needed. They learned that while strategy is important, execution is everything.

Knowing the value of the team, they learned the unwritten rules and how to play the game. Setting goals and creating an organizational mission and vision were keys to success. Once created, this mission needed to be clearly articulated.

The MPW found they had to let go of perfectionism. Business is a collaborative process, and these women were quick to realize that they couldn't do everything themselves. They learned they needed to be close to the mark in their decisions but not unfailingly perfect. They learned to delegate, and they learned to pick their battles carefully, choosing only the ideas, projects, and people that they were willing to back and protect. They also learned that when they made mistakes or suffered a failure, they had to learn from the experience, take the next step forward, and bring their team along with them.

Balance was important. First, there was the need to find a balance between their feminine and masculine traits. To excel meant being results-oriented and goal-oriented (typically masculine traits) and still display a high degree of social skills (typically feminine). Second, they tried to find a balance between their work and the other important things in their lives. Devotion to family allowed them to persevere during the most challenging times at work. And being able to enjoy breaks from work helped them rejuvenate themselves.

Top Ten Success Nuggets

The following is a distillation of the lessons learned and advice that will allow you to be successful.

#1 Success Nugget: Attitude Is Everything

All of the women mentioned the importance of attitude. Success is a mindset. How can you keep an attitude that will allow you to persevere even when things are not going well, when you're overwhelmed, or when someone is blocking you? One of Liz Fetter's secrets is using inspirational quotes that she repeats to herself. Her favorite is: *"If you know how to swim, it doesn't matter how deep the water is."*

Everyday, every moment we are deciding how we want to feel, think, and act. This is our own personal choice, not anyone else's. This is the one thing that we have total control over in our lives. The *only* thing! What decisions and choices will you make from this moment forward? Will you choose to love life, grow and prosper, feel terrific about who you are and what you are capable of? The freedom to choose is yours. (A list of motivational questions you might want to consider posting on your mirror is in Appendix B.)

#2 Success Nugget: People Skills Are Paramount

Your employees get you promoted, and your peers allow you to be promoted. That, according to the MPW, underscores the importance of getting along with others. Great people skills are required to be an effective leader and to advance in an organization.

Empathy is essential. You need employees to respect you if you are going to be able to lead them. That respect comes from your ability to understand others, being fair and even-minded, and valuing and respecting the opinions of others. The MPW found they had to be tolerant of others, understand where they are coming from, and withhold judgment about them until they could think about the motivations involved. This same empathy is used when making presentations. The MPW adjust their communications based on the audience they are speaking to.

Another important people skill for these powerful women was listening. The higher they climbed up the ladder, the more important listening became. The MPW rated it a "10" on a scale of 1-to-10 of the skills most needed for success. Similarly, the MPW learned to show trust in their subordinates. The women acquired the ability to delegate and then to trust the subordinates to do the job.

Being a leader means being watched all of the time. Thus, said the MPW, they needed to be aware of the impact of what they said and did. Employees watched what the MPW *did* more than they listened to what the women *said*. Employees expected them to show leadership and confidence.

To advance means adapting to the environment of the organization. This does not mean changing your personal core. If your values are not the same as the organization, then you need to leave.

#3 Success Nugget: Build a Winning Team

These women found it was important to surround themselves with the best and the brightest. The MPW had so much confidence in themselves that they weren't concerned with whether their subordinates will outshine them or take their jobs. In fact, having very able people beneath them made it easier to replace themselves as they advanced.

They also found it is important to hire people who complemented their strengths and weaknesses. While they wanted subordinates who shared their same philosophies, values, goals and standards, the MPW also needed a diverse team. When coming into a new organization, having a mix of new and experienced employees gave a mixture of perspectives.

Ann Sweeney hires people who are courageous and willing to say "Why not?" She wants people who will think outside of the box and are willing to take risks.

The women learned that you can build a culture in a portion of the company. You do not need to be leading the company to make a difference. You can influence a part of the organization and make it the way you want it to be.

Karen Garrison rates performance levels with an A, B, C, or D. By hiring the best, you end up with A players on your team. Karen talked about the fact that employees are not always A players, that sometimes they will fall to a B or even a C level. You need to know where people are in the stages of their lives, what their priorities are, and what personal issues they may be dealing with. When someone is a D player, they need to be given feedback about their performance and if it doesn't improve, that person should move on to someplace where they can perform better.

Part of the key to keeping people on track is to give them regular feedback on how they are performing in relationship to the goals of the organization. Also let them know how the organization is doing and how they can contribute to its success. Allow them to develop their own action plans.

Recognizing people who do good work is a key to a motivated team. Even a simple gesture like a "thank you" or spending a little personal time with them can make a lot of difference. You can draw people to a team by recognizing them for what they do well and what they like to do, and then giving them the chance to do so.

#4 Success Nugget: Be Who You Are

The MPW did not change their values. Instead, they learned how to polish their behavior and still remain true to themselves. Ursula Burns learned, *"You have to figure out a way to temper yourself to be effective without changing who you are."* Workers need to see such consistency in their leaders. This gives them security and fosters trust. So if the leader is not true to who she is, her subordinates won't be, either.

When they started, these women executives adjusted their behavior and the way they dressed to fit the environment. They found out quickly that they could only go so far outside the boundaries of the corporate cultures and expectations before it would hinder their careers. They found ways to adjust so they didn't feel like they were changing the core of who they were but were still doing what's right for them. To excel you need to find a fit into a culture that matches who you are.

Several women commented on the need to temper their enthusiasm or aggressiveness. Aggressiveness in women can be considered pushy and overwhelming by some people. The MPW monitored people's reactions and then adjusted their approach in a way that allowed them to fit in and be listened to. Know the environment you are in and what is acceptable. Dress and act in the manner of the position that you want to reach, not the one you occupy now.

Think about: What will make you happy? How willing are you to adapt to the environment? What will adapting mean to you? What are the most important things in life to you?

Only by understanding yourself and what makes you tick will you be confident and portray the image you desire. If you question yourself, others will also. By understanding your values, you will know when you have reached a point of saying this organization no longer works for me. Otherwise, you may get frustrated or stay longer than is good for your career.

You will find that your tastes and styles change over time. Figuring out who you are is an ongoing and growing process. The most important thing is to be who you are, sticking by your values, believing in yourself, being happy, passionate about what you are doing and going for what you want in life.

#5 Success Nugget: Take Charge of Your Career

Only if you take action will your career be advanced. Here are some career-furthering ideas:

1) Stand out and be noticed. It's not enough to just prove yourself technically in your field, such as sales, computer graphics, marketing, or financial planning. You must also:

> • Be the best at what you do. Your results must be exceptional for the company to truly value what you are doing.

> • Develop your career plan, and discuss your career aspirations with your manager.

> • Keep your manager and upper management up to date on your contributions and accomplishments. You are responsible for managing your boss.

> • Talk to upper management when you get an opportunity. Make sure they know who you are, but leave the right impression.

• Take an active part in your evaluations. Writing them yourself gives you the best opportunity to make sure that all your "good points" are raised. Also, be aware of where you need improvement and discuss with your boss how you can get the skills you need.

• Find out if your company has a "Fast Track" program for high-potential individuals. Some companies have programs to send their "high potentials" to executive programs at certain universities, such as Stanford. Ask what it would take to be part of the programs available.

• Think about how you can add value to the organization. Take active steps in that direction.

• Write articles for the company newspaper or other periodicals. Are there places you can speak for the company?

2) Write down your goals. Where do you want to be in five, 10, or 15 years? The more specific you can be, the better. And the more you can visualize where you want to be, the better your chances are of getting there.

3) Decide if you need to make a career change. A number of the MPW wished they had accelerated their careers by making a change earlier than they did. Ask yourself:

• Where am I? How long have I been here? (Normally, within 18 months you should be able to master an assignment.) What would have to happen for me to move forward from here? Tolerate shorter-term inconveniences, but stay focused on the longer-term goals.

- Look out two positions from where you are and assess whether that is where you want to be. Several MPW said that is an excellent way to plan. Consider working for the person who has the job you want to determine if that is really the job for you. Look for positions that allow you to watch how things are done in the company.

- If you determine your organization isn't supporting you, get out! It is easy to get emotionally tied to your work and hope the situation will change when it won't.

- Decide if the corporate culture fits your personality style, standards, ethics or values? Look for a culture and job match that will allow you to succeed. Remember, you are in control of your career.

- Learn whose support you need to help achieve your goals. Build a support network that can directly or indirectly help you.

- Figure out what you need to reach your goal, such as a degree or a certain kind of experience? Each career move should add to your skill portfolio.

4) Find a Mentor. Several of the MPW found mentors within their companies who helped them advance more quickly.

- Look for someone within the organization who represents your values.

- A mentor can be a man or woman, and the relationship can be formal or informal.

- Mentoring works best when it is a personal experience, not an assignment.

5) Learn all you can about your business or industry.

● Ask for an assignment to a different work group. Within most organizations, knowing various areas of the business is a prerequisite for a move into the executive ranks. You may be able to move close to the top as a specialist, but most organizations will not give you a policy- or decision-making position without knowledge of other areas of the business. The exception to this seems to be Finance. People have been able to move up the financial ranks and move directly into an operations executive position.

● Volunteer for new teams and task forces. Expand your knowledge base and do networking simultaneously.

● Read the annual report. A copy can be obtained from the Investors Relations department. The report will identify what is important to the company. Most companies are driven by events that impact their stockholders.

#6 Success Nugget: Grow or Die

All the MPW took on the responsibility to be a change agent for their organizations. They put themselves out there and said, "Yes, I can do it!" That takes courage. We all have that courage inside of us, but we just don't recognize it sometimes. Reach inside yourself and do what is necessary to achieve the happiness and fulfillment you deserve.

Only by taking risks do we grow and achieve success. By immersing yourself in the challenge you face, you will be concentrating on what needs to be done instead of focusing on your fears. We have the emotion of fear to protect ourselves from harm. But it can get in our way if we allow it to limit us from being our best and getting what we truly want out of life.

By taking risks, you are saying "I'm prepared to fail, to make mistakes, because that is a reality." Whatever you set your sights on is what you will achieve. If you set the limit low, that's probably as far as you will go. The mind only knows what you tell it. It has no sense of the truth. The truth is what you tell it. If you think you can or can't, you're right.

The risks you take are a direct correlation to your belief in yourself. By taking a risk, you show the faith and confidence you have in yourself.

You can't avoid the hard decisions in life. You can postpone them but eventually they have to be faced. Isn't making such a choice better when done early rather than torturing yourself over a decision you can't run from? Do you need additional information to make a decision? Where can you get some advice? Sometimes, people are reluctant to ask for help. When you work through something and take the risk, you become stronger.

Jean Hamilton makes an excellent point about how having the passion allows you to push forward, to take the leap to what you know is right in your heart. If you don't have that passion, *"when it comes time to make the tough decisions, you'll be afraid to make them. You won't do what you know has to be done because you don't feel it in your heart. You won't be willing to take the risk and say this is what has to be done for the business; this is the right thing to do."*

#7 Success Nugget: Choose Your Priorities Early - Family and/or Career

The biggest challenge these women face is how to balance time with their family, friends, and career. They are, or want to be, a wife. Most of them want to be, or are, mothers. But how do they fit these roles into their schedules? Time is so precious to them. How do they reconcile their family aspirations with their career aspirations?

For starters, they all got their families to agree on what the priorities should be. Support from their family had to be there if they were going to work such long hours and travel. When these women had children, they found they had to re-balance their lives so they had the time to spend with the kids. They made the decision that their families are their number one priority. No one will ever say at the end of their life, "I wish I had spent more time at work."

Most of the women put off having children when they began their careers. For some, that postponement may mean they never will have children. Several of the women commented that if they had realized how easy it was to re-balance their lives, they would have had children earlier. They were willing to do what was necessary to get what they want. They figured out how to make it work.

Everyone has to prioritize their own lives and decide what is most important to them. Where do you want to spend your time and energy? How important is your career in the scheme of your life? How do you define success? You hear of increasing numbers of women who reach the pinnacle of their careers and decide it's time for another stage in their lives. They quit their jobs, start a family, and stay at home for a while. Others start businesses out of their home so they can be with their children. What is right for one person is not right for another. Only you can set your priorities.

Deciding early in your career what is most important will help guide your career. Some companies are reluctant to support a woman's career advancement if they don't know her goals. Therefore, once you know what you want, communicate it to your management and get its support.

The MPW gave their family priority and made that known to their management. If they could not go to all their children's events, they chose the important ones. If that was not O.K. with the firm, then they were not working in a company that supported their values.

What effect will having children have on your life? On the time you have to spend with other family members and friends? Also, think about how much time would you want to take off when you have a child? Do you want to come back to work full-time? What support system exists that can help you? Will you need to leave work at 5:00? If so, will that allow you to get the work done? If not, are you willing to take it home and do it there? Can you? How much control do you have over your workload? Do you have access to technology at home?

Most of these women travel extensively. Mary Farrell made a decision that she would not be available for global travel. That affected her career, and she understood that. Will you need to travel? How much and for how long? What effect will being on the road have on your family?

Different jobs have different requirements. Mary found that by moving to research she was better able to achieve her goals. Study your field to see if it meets your future goals and aspirations. Be realistic about what career choices you make based on your values and priorities.

We all make sacrifices to get what we want. Most of these women do not sleep eight hours. They have either decided that getting the work done is more important or they don't need that much sleep. Many of them work on weekends or at least attend to their in-basket, emails or voicemails then. This is a choice they make to have what they want. You may not want to make it to the very top, but think about where you want to go and what will it take to get there? What choices and sacrifices do you need to make to achieve your goals?

#8 Success Nugget: Know Your Geographic Limits - To Move or Not to Move

The decision to move or not had a big impact on these women's lives. Think about this issue early in your career and discuss your preferences with friends, family, and management. This will allow for a smoother transition when the time comes and could determine your career direction.

When seeking a job elsewhere, or if a job at a different location in your firm opens, you can save time and energy if you have already prioritized your personal needs. To do that, consider:

• Where are you willing to move to or live? Take into account weather, rural vs. urban environments, social preferences, and so on.

• If your company has a corporate headquarters elsewhere, are you willing to move there at some point in your career?

• Are you willing to move to get additional experience or exposure?

• What impact will moving have on your family and friends?

• How will you feel moving away from your established life?

• Is your spouse or Significant Other able to pick up and move with you?

• Will your company find a job for him/her?

• How will he/she feel about being a trailing spouse or Significant Other?

• How will your children be affected by a move? If it is mid-school year, how will you handle it?

• What will you do if your children don't want to go?

• Family and friends may or may not be supportive. How important is that to you?

If you are not yet romantically attached, you may want to make mobility a consideration for those you get involved with. If you are attached, start the communication process now to get their opinions and options before the situation arises.

Moving your children can either be the easiest or the toughest part of the move. Start the communication early, even if you may not yet be moving. Get their views and worries out in the open as well as any benefits. Getting your family to buy in early to the need for moving can make them feel valued and will lessen their fears.

#9 Success Nugget: Think Outside of the Box

All these women love challenges and believe as Anne Sweeney does that "Life is an adventure." They never want to look back and have regrets and wonder "what if." They love creating something out of nothing. They are naturally curious as to what is on the other side of a challenge, how to reach that goal, what they need to know and learn?

Mary Farrell found that being ambitious enabled her to work around a "no" answer. Men have learned this lesson well and consider "no" to just be a postponement until they figure another way around the situation. These women, too, have figured out how to navigate around obstacles to achieve their goals. Having goals and a vision makes you unstoppable.

When you use questioning skills it enables you to see things in a different way, from a different angle or from someone else's perspective. Try to look at things as if you were seeing them for the first time. Be open to new ideas. Truly listen to what others have to say.

#10 Success Nugget: Push Beyond Your Limits

The MPW found that each time they pushed past their limits, whole new areas opened up for them. Each time they got beyond their fear, they saw they were capable of even more.

When these women set their minds to something, there is no stopping them. They believe they can achieve anything and that failure is not an option. However, if they do fail at something, they ask what they can learn from the situation, make a mental note to do something different the next time, and move on.

Think about: What limits do you set on your capabilities? What are the boundaries you set for yourself? What do you say to yourself about your capabilities? If you were to push past your fear of doing something, what would happen?

Usually, the worst things that can ever happen to us if we venture beyond our comfort level is that we fail, are told "no," or make a mistake. Those are also growth opportunities. Remember: It is only your response to a situation that determines the meaning of it. You can choose to learn from it and move on, or feel like a victim. You can convince yourself that you are a failure, or merely that you failed.

You are capable of accomplishing anything you have a deep desire and passion for, believe that you can have, and are willing to take the actions necessary to get. Life is yours to make it what you want it to be. Use your mind, heart and instincts to determine the direction that is right for you. Take the risks, stretch to reach your full potential, and always be true to yourself.

Actions and Attributes of the Most Powerful Women

These actions and attributes are the key elements of their success. Review this checklist to determine which characteristics you have or need. Think about what you would need to do to acquire these qualities, which have been categorized for ease of identification.

Do I have these characteristics and attitudes?	Have	Need

Achievement

	Have	Need
1. College degree or advanced degrees		
2. Consistently exceed expectations		
3. Understand and play by the corporate unwritten rules		
4. Focus on the goal or objective – pick what is most important.		
5. Constantly are raising their goals		
6. Set expectations for themselves and their team		
7. Strive to be the best they can be		
8. Make a difference in whatever they are doing		
9. Visionary		
10. Results-oriented		

Attitude

	Have	Need
11. An attitude of success		
12. Incredible self-confidence - Believe in themselves and their capabilities		
13. Persevering, tenacious		
14. Don't let personal comments from others affect their performance		
15. View life as an adventure		
16. Possess a high energy level		

17. Passion for what they do
18. Take responsibility for their actions and choices
19. Being who they are
20. Open to new ideas
21. Love challenges
22. Tolerate shorter term inconveniences and stay longer-term focused
23. Have a sense of humor
24. Deliberate
25. Flexible
26. High integrity

Self Improvement
27. Most of their training was on the job experience
28. Learned from the people around them and then used it in their own lives
29. Learned from their own mistakes or failures, let it go, and moved on
30. Life-long learners
31. Re-evaluate along the way and then adjust their path accordingly

Skills
32. Know how to get things done
33. Know what skills they have and reach out for those they need
34. Delegate well
35. Developed styles that men are comfortable with
36. Make decisive decisions
37. Great communicators-honed their interpersonal skills, especially the ability to listen

38. Use their intuition
39. Opinion leaders
40. Problem solvers
41. Strategic thinkers
42. Effective leaders
43. Effective presentation skills – presenting well-organized facts, slanting the presentation to the particular audience, and thinking ahead to what questions will be asked
44. Changed their skill sets as the moved up the ladder; polished their skills as they advanced in their careers
45. Identified their accomplishments to others
46. Powerful networkers

Style
47. Respect others and value their opinions
48. Risk takers
49. Teamwork and building a winning team is a critical element in their success
50. In the early part of their career, their focus and priority was learning and mastering the business even if it meant working long hours
51. Customer-focused
52. Collaborative
53. Recognize their employees for a job well done

Personal
54. Family comes first
55. Willingness to show they care
56. Have a great support system of people who support their lifestyle and career choices
57. Made sacrifices of sleep and personal time in order to get where they wanted to go

58. Sought balance by carving out enough time for themselves

59. Courageous

60. Willing to relocate to reach their goals

QUESTIONS FOR REFLECTION

Morning Questions

1. What am I happy about in my life right now?

2. What am I excited about in my life right now?

3. What am I proud of in my life right now?

4. What am I grateful for in my life right now?

5. What am I committed to in my life right now?

6. Whom do I most enjoy being with today?

7. What do I love?

8. Who loves me?

Evening Questions

1. What have I accomplished today?

2. What have I learned today?

3. How did I grow today?

4. What have I done today to help, be kind, or be thankful to someone else?

5. What step or steps have I taken today to reach my goals?

6. Did I make mistakes today or fail? If so, what can I learn from it? What would have to happen for me to decide to learn from it and then let it go?

7. How have I celebrated my successes today?

Questions That Create Success

1. Did I give or am I giving my full effort? If not, what do I need to do at this moment or the next time the situation arises to give my full effort? If I were to give my full effort, what would happen?

2. Did I learn or am I learning something? What would have to happen for me to start learning now? If I begin learning now, what will happen?

3. If some situation has not turned out the way I wanted, I need to ask myself:

    Am I taking responsibility for my action?

    Could there be another interpretation of the situation?

    Is it possible that someone meant something different than the way I took it?

    Am I taking the situation personally?

    Is the conversation I'm having with myself one of love and caring?

    What action could I take now to resolve or change the situation?

Companies With High Percentages of Women Corporate Officers, Women Line Officers and Women Top Earners

Fourteen companies in the Fortune 500 that rank favorably in three key metrics measured by Catalyst in 1999:

1) Corporate officers
2) Line positions
3) Top earners

These 14 companies all have at least:

- 35% women corporate officers
- 15% women line
- At least one woman among the top five wage earners

> Avon
> BJ's Wholesale Club
> Dayton Hudson
> Enron
> Hannaford Brothers
> Kelly Services
> Knight Ridder
> Mattel
> PaineWebber
> SLM Holding
> Solectron
> Southwest Airlines
> Times Mirror (now part of the Tribune Co.)
> Washington Mutual

Best and Worst Industries for Women

In 1999, Catalyst provided the following statistics:

<u>Highest Percentages of Women Corporate Officers</u>

Industry	Number of Companies	Percent of Women Corporate Officers
Diversified financials	8	27.1%
Transportation equipment	1	25.0%
Toys, sporting goods	2	24.1%
Publishing, printing	7	24.1%
Tobacco	2	20.8%

<u>Lowest percentages of Women Corporate Officers</u>

Industry	Number of Companies	Percentage of Women Corporate Officers
Mining, crude-oil	2	3.7%
Computer peripherals	5	3.3%
Waste management	2	2.8%
Textiles	1	0.0%
Trucking	2	0.0%

Biographical Summaries of the Most Powerful Women

Shelley G. Broader

1997 – Present	Vice President, Perishables Merchandising – Hannaford Bros.
1996 – 1997	Director, Perishables Merchandising – Hannaford Bros.
1995 – 1996	District Manager – Hannaford Bros.
1994 – 1995	New York Merchandising/Buyer – Hannaford Bros.
1993 – 1994	Operations Coordinator, New York Distribution Center – Hannaford Bros.
1991 – 1992	Store Manager – Hannaford Bros.
1989 – 1991	Associate Vice President - First Albany Corporation
1987 – 1989	Inside Wholesaler – Massachusetts Financial Services

Organizational Affiliations and Awards

Board member
Main Coalition for Excellence in Education

Ursula Burns - All positions held at Xerox Corporation

2000 – Present	Senior Corporate Vice President and Vice President, Worldwide Manufacturing Operations
1997 - 2000	Vice President and General Manager, Departmental Business Unit

1995 - 1997	Vice President and General Manager, Work Group Copier Business
1993 - 1995	Vice President and General Manager, Office Network Copying Business Team
1992 - 1993	Vice President and General Manager, Office Color and Facsimile Business
1990 - 1992	Executive Assistant
1980 - 1990	Mechanical Engineering summer intern, Engineering - Manager, low volume business planning; systems engineering manager; high-volume product development

Organizational Affiliations and Awards

Executive board, PQ Corporation
Executive board, Hunt Corporation
Executive board, Lincoln Electric Corporation

Board of Directors
FIRST
Allendale Columbia School Board
Boy Scouts of America
University of Rochester Medical School

Mary C. Farrell

| 1982 - Present | Senior Investment Strategist and Managing Director - PaineWebber Smith Barney and Merrill Lynch. |
| 1971 - | Pershing & Company. |

Organizational Affiliations and Awards

Member, Financial Women's Association
Board of Directors, Women's Economic Round Table
Elected to *Wall $treet Week With Louis Rukeyser* Hall of Fame
Board of Overseers, New York University's Stern School of
    Business
Board of Directors, Mitchell Hutchins Asset Management
Member, PaineWebber Diversity Council
Alumni Meritorious Service Award, New York University Alumni
    Association, 1999

Elizabeth Fetter

2000 – Present	President and Chief Executive Officer – NorthPoint Communications
1999 – 1999	President and Chief Operating Officer – NorthPoint Communications
1998 – 1999	Vice President and General Manager of the Consumer Services Group - US WEST
1997 - 1998	Vice President and General Manager, Operator and Directory Services - SBC Communications
1995 – 1997	President, Industry Markets Group – Pacific Bell
1994 – 1995	Vice President, Industry Markets, Pacific Bell
1994 – 1994	Vice President , Marketing Services,– Pacific Bell
1993 - 1994	Area Vice President Sales, North Coast Business Unit – Pacific Bell
1992 – 1993	Executive Director, Financial Strategy & Analysis – Pacific Bell
1991 – 1992	Executive Director, Strategic Planning – Pacific Bell

1990 – 1991	Senior Manager – Marakon Associates
1988 – 1990	Manager – Marakon Associates
1987 – 1988	Associate – Marakon Associates
1982 – 1987	Variety of financial and strategic positions – Chevron Corp.

Organizational Affiliations and Awards

Boards
Andrew Corp., Board of Directors
Berbee Inc., Board of Directors
Datum Inc., Board of Directors
General Magic, Board of Directors
Global Asset Management, Advisory Board
Executive Women's Alliance, Advisory Board
Car-List, Advisory Board

Affiliations
ATHENA
Women's Forum West
Young President's Organization
San Francis City Club
MENTITIUM 100
Charter 100
World Affairs Council
International Engineering Consortium

Recent Awards
Appointed to Women's Forum West
Named Woman of the Year, Bronx-Lebanon Hospital
Appointed by University President to lifetime honor of Alumni
    Fellow, Penn State University
"Breakthrough Award" for business and community leadership in
    Northern California

Named one of 20 "Bay Area's Most Powerful Corporate Women"
Named one of the top 50 Bay Area businesswomen, Bay Area
Asian Employee Group Leadership Award, Pacific Bell
MWBE/DVBE Leadership Award, Pacific Bell

Karen M. Garrison – Positions held at Pitney Bowes, Dictaphone,
and its subsidiary

1999 – Present	President of Pitney Bowes Management Services
1997 - 1999	Executive Director of Admin. Services
1995 - 1997	Vice President, Customer Support Ops.
1994 – 1995	Vice President, Customer Service
1992 – 1994	Vice President, Finance and Chief Financial Officer.
1977 – 1992	World-Wide Controller and Factory Ops.

Jean Hamilton

1998 – Present	Chief Executive Officer – Prudential Institutional and Executive Vice President, The Prudential Insurance Company of America
1995 – 1998	President – Prudential Diversified Group
1992 – 1995	President – Prudential Capital Group
1991 – 1992	Senior Vice President – Prudential Capital Corp.
1988 – 1991	President – Prudential Asset Sales & Syndication's, Inc.
1971 – 1988	Senior Vice President – First National Bank of Chicago (Head of Northeastern Banking Group)

1970 – 1971	Sales – Management Assistance Corporation
1968 – 1970	Marketing Research/Product Development – Continental Illinois Bank & Trust

Organizational Affiliations and Awards

Board Member
The Prudential Foundation
Independent College Fund of New Jersey
Women's Economic Round Table
Four Nations, Standing Tall
Grass Roots

Ellen Hancock

2000 – Present	Chairman and Chief Executive Officer – Exodus Communications
1998 – 2000	President and Chief Executive Officer – Exodus Communications
1996 - 1998	Executive Vice President, R&D and Chief Technology Officer – Apple Computer
1995 - 1996	Senior Vice President and Chief Operating Officer - National Semiconductor
- 1995	Senior Vice President and Group Executive Networking Hardware Division - IBM
1992 -	Senior Vice President – IBM
1985	Vice President - IBM

Organizational Affiliations and Awards

Board of Directors
Colgate Palmolive,
Aetna

Marist College

Member of the Council on Foreign Relations
Member of the Committee of 200 (Women Executives)
Honorary Doctorate of Humane Letters from the State University
    of Western Connecticut.

Anne Livermore – All positions held at Hewlett Packard

1999 - Present	President Enterprise and Commercial Business and HP Vice President, member of the Executive Council
1998 - 1999	General Manager, Enterprise Computing Solutions Organization
1997 - 1998	General Manager, Software & Services Grp.
1996 - 1997	General Manager, Worldwide Customer Support Operations
1995 - 1996	Corporate Vice President
1991 - 1995	Marketing Manager, Professional Services
1989 - 1991	Marketing Manager, Application Support
1986 - 1989	Research and Development Manager, Application Support Division
1985 - 1986	Marketing Services Manager, Application Support Division
1982 - 1985	Working on administration processes and systems in the U.S. Field Operations

Organizational Affiliations and Awards

United Parcel Service (UPS) Board of Directors
Board of Visitors, Kenan-Flagler Business School at the University
    of North Carolina

Named by *Fortune* Magazine as the 13th most powerful woman in
business in 1999

Anne Sweeney

1998 – Present	President, Disney/ABC Cable Networks, President, Disney Channel
1996 – 1998	Executive Vice President, Disney/ABC Cable Networks and President, Disney Channel
1993 – 1996	Chairman and Chief Executive Officer – FX Networks
1981 - 1993	Senior Vice President, Program Enterprises - Nickelodeon

Organizational Affiliations and Awards

Board Member
National Association of Television Program Executives
Walter Kaitz Foundation
Honorary chair of Cable Positive
Women in Cable
Special Olympics

Awards
Woman of the Year – Women in Cable
Advocate Leader Award – Women in Cable
Inducted into the American Advertising Federation's Advertising
Hall of Achievement
Honored by Girls, Inc.
Joel A. Berger Award – Cable Positive
H.E.L.P. Group Humanitarian Award
Named 47th most powerful woman by *Fortune* Magazine in 1998

BIBLIOGRAPHY

[1] Catalyst is a nonprofit research and advisory services organization that works with business to advance women

[2] *1999 Catalyst Census of Women Corporate Officers and Top Wage Earners*, Catalyst, 1999.

[3] *1998 Catalyst Census of Women Corporate Officers and Top Wage Earners*, Catalyst, 1998.

[4] *20 Facts on Women Workers,* U.S. Department of Labor: Women's Bureau, 1999.

[5] *Report on American Workforce 1999,* U.S. Department of Labor, Bureau of Labor Statistics, 1999

[6] Popcorn, Faith. *EVEolution : The Eight Truths of Marketing to Women, 2000*

[7] *Women in Corporate Leadership Progress and Prospects*, New York: Catalyst, 1996

[8] *Women in Corporate Leadership: Progress and Prospects*, New York: Catalyst, 1996.

[9] www.catalystwomen.org

[10] Korabik, K. "Androgyny and Leadership Style," *Journal of Business Ethics,* 1990.

[11] Helegesen, Sally. *The Female Advantage: Women's Ways of Leadership*, New York: Doubleday, 1990.

[12] Aburdene, Patricia, and Naisbitt, John. *Megatrends for Women*, 1st ed. New York: Villard Books, 1992.

[13] Helgesen, Sally. *The Female Advantage: Women's Ways of Leadership*, New York: Doubleday, 1990.

[14] Hite, Shere. *Sex & Business,*. New York: Prentice Hall, 2000.

ACKNOWLEDGMENTS

I am deeply grateful to the 10 gracious women who made the time to participate in the book project and were willing to share their stories. Without their openness, commitment and success, this book would not be possible. Not only are their stories fascinating but it was such a pleasure to spend time with them. I sincerely thank Anne Sweeney, Ann Livermore, Ellen Hancock, Jean Hamilton, Karen Garrison, Liz Fetter, Mary Farrell, Ursula Burns, and Shelley Broader.

Another powerful women, Janice Roberts, took the time out of her busy schedule to write a fabulous Foreword that enhanced the rest of the book.

My husband has provided unwavering support, encouragement, and was the pillar stone for the project. Thank you for supporting me in the pursuit of my dreams.

Several people who truly believed in my capabilities and me were Ernie Jones, Carol Sorrick, Liz Fetter, and Diana Wenman. They share the desire to empower other people to be the best they can be.

The administrative assistants and Public Relations departments at the interviewees' firms worked tirelessly to coordinate with these busy women's schedules, provide the information I needed to complete the book, and make my life a lot easier.

Special thanks to Greg Scott and Lindsey Burroughs of GTE, Ellen Hancock, Denis Waitley, Mark Victor Hansen, and Gerry Laybourne for their belief in and endorsement of this project.

As I began to put my acknowledgments on paper, I realized how many people had contributed in one way or another, and I appreciate the time and help everyone gave me. Special thanks to my parents and father-in-law Alex Pestrak for their ongoing belief in me. Mike Pestrak, Mike Smith, John Harrison,

Larry Wiese, Tony Dohrmann, Vincent Molina, and Jim Burk for their special advice and support of the project. And to my special friend Ab Mobasher for always being there for me.

John Chen, Roger Essen, and Mistie Shaw provided extra effort to see this project a success. For my special friends Dale Fetherling, Suzy Beemer, Debbie Bermont, Rose Quezada, Colette Murray, Susan Pestrak, Sara Wilensky, Sheryl Roush, and Patti Thomma for the dedication and time in reviewing the book drafts.

In the long effort to find the "right" title, thanks go to Liz Fetter, Jim Cathcart, Charlene Kennedy, Dave Morton, Susan Snow, Jane Netherton, Kim Brown, NSA focus group, Willeen Hasler, Deborah Lee Stangoni, and Chris Witt for providing their creative ideas.

Thanks to Betsie Brown, Brooke Halpin, Barbara Monteiro, and Lucy Jo Palladino for their advice and insights on publicity. Dan Poynter, Gordon Jackson, Greg Godek, Howie Smith, Deb Werksman, Ed Helvey, Roger Herman, Cynthia Kersey, and Mark LeBlanc for their book publishing advice. Lauren Herko, Sara Hume, Kristen Timothy, and Carmen Butler, who provided invaluable referrals.

The Income Builders International seminar allowed me to understand that this project was bigger than a book and that I could figure out a way to accomplish it.

A special acknowledgement goes out for the work that the Catalyst organization has done in support of women. Without its research, we would not know the status of women leaders in Fortune 500 companies.

ABOUT THE AUTHOR

Debra Pestrak is CEO of Success UNleashed, Inc. As an inspiring, award-winning motivational speaker, business consultant, educator and coach she delivers high-impact, results oriented, and empowering seminars. Debra works with corporations and individuals that want to increase sales, improve teaming, identify and foster leadership, and retain customers and employees. Her seminars provide key skills on peak performance, attitude, success thinking, and relationship and influencing skills.

Seminar topics: *Success Secrets of the Most Powerful Women in Business, Getting What You Want Through the Art of Influence, "Power" Yourself for Success* and *The Winning Difference: How to Overcome Obstacles.* Debra's talks are energized, interactive, personalized and practical.

Ms. Pestrak has a degree in Business Administration and Management, and extensive experience in Neuro Linguistic Programming (NLP). Her success in corporate America enabled her to speak to and relate one-on-one with these women CEOs, Presidents and other corporate officers to capture their insights.

Want to empower your people for greater success? Then call Debra toll free at 888-786-3777 today or visit her website at www.DebraPestrak.com.

Remember to order your audio or video copies of these interviews at www.MostPowerfulWomen.com, at the back of this book or at the toll free number. Look for the upcoming television programming based on these interviews and further books on the MPW.

My passion is to make a difference in others lives. I would love to hear your story about how this book has changed your life. Please email me at debra@DebraPestrak.com.

INDEX

VISIT US AT

www.MostPowerfulWomen.com

Gifts for your friends

Order this book from your local bookstore or web-store. Orders may also be placed with Success UNleashed, Inc.

Fax orders: 760-434-7076. Send this form.

Telephone orders: Call 888-786-3777 toll free or 760-434-3343. Have your credit card ready.

Email orders: Go to website www.MostPowerfulWomen.com.

Postal orders: Success UNleashed, 300 Carlsbad Village Drive, Suite 108A-78, Carlsbad, CA 92008. USA

Please send the following books, audio or videos. I understand that I may return any of them for a full refund-for any reason, no questions asked.

___ Copies of *Playing with the Big Boys* **Book** $25.95 each

Success Secrets of the Most Powerful Women in Business

___ **Success Package** $269 ($490 retail value), includes 9 tape video

set, audio tape album and copy of *Playing with the Big Boys* book

___ **Audio Tape Album** $99 ($175 retail value), includes book

___ **CD Audio Album** $119 ($195 retail value), includes book

___ **Video Set** (9 videos) $199 ($341 retail value) includes book

Quantity discounts available.

Shipping: _____ 1st book $5, each additional book $2.50, Audio album $7, Video set $17, Package $20. International: $9 for first book, call for other rates.

Sales Tax: _____ Add 7.75% sales tax for orders to California addresses.

Total order $_____

Contact Success UNleashed (888-786-3777) for leader-led training packages on instilling success traits in your team.

Please Print

Name:_____

Address:_____

City:_____ State:_____ Zip:_____ Country: _____

Telephone _____ Email address _____

Credit Card: Visa MC AMX Nbr._____

Signature: _____ Exp. Date: _____